OUR STORY

OUR STORY

*77 Hours That Tested Our
Friendship and Our Faith*

•

The Quecreek Miners
AS TOLD TO JEFF GOODELL

HYPERION

NEW YORK

ISBN: 0-7868-9065-7

Hyperion books are available for special promotions and premiums. For details contact Hyperion Special Markets, 77 West 66th Street, 11th floor, New York, New York 10023, or call 212-456-0133.

FIRST MASS MARKET EDITION

10 9 8 7 6 5 4 3 2 1

ACKNOWLEDGMENTS

We are all profoundly grateful to the rescue workers, volunteers, friends, family, and citizens of Somerset County who helped give this story a happy ending. Also, thanks to Larry Sanitsky, Elwood Reid, Will Schwalbe, Leslie Wells, Heather Schroder, Mitch Gelman, Carolyn Chriss, Carol Raben, David Malley, Jon and Margot Knupp, Tina Kruger, Bill Krietz, Susan Romans, Michele, Milo, Georgia, and, especially, Grace.

CONTENTS

One
The Last Cut   1

Two
Coal Country   5

Three
A World of Water   17

Four
Going Underground   29

Five
Battle on the Beltway   37

Six
The Call   45

Seven
Rescuing Moe   53

Eight
Building Walls   77

Nine
Sipesville   89

Ten
Swamped   102

Eleven
How to Drown with Dignity   109

Twelve
Drilling and Pumping   123

Thirteen
Roughing It   135

Fourteen
We Dropped the Bit   152

Fifteen
Visions of Acosta   166

Sixteen
The Longest Day   176

Seventeen
Who Wants to Go Home?   191

Eighteen
Born Again   202

Nineteen
Reunion   218

OUR STORY

I · THE LAST CUT

At about 9 p.m. on Wednesday, July 24, 2002, Mark Popernack, who goes by the nickname Moe, was a mile and a half underground in the Quecreek mine outside of Somerset, Pennsylvania. As was often the case, Moe was at the controls of a big machine called a miner—a long, low, heavy tractor with an eleven-and-a-half-foot-wide carbide-steel cutter head up front that looks like an enormous buzz saw. The cutter head rips through the coal seam as easily as a Weedwacker through grass, pulverizing the ancient black rock and sending it shooting out the back of the miner onto waiting shuttle cars. The miner is the biggest, baddest machine in the mine, an earth-devouring monster.

As an operator of the miner, Moe is among the best in the business. He's forty-one, wiry and strong, with short dark hair, an angular face, and shrewd green eyes. He's a third-generation coal miner, and has worked underground for more than twenty years, many of them running the miner. He knows all the machine's tricks. He can tell by the sound of the miner's carbide teeth digging into the coal seam if he is cutting too high or too low; he knows how to guide the machine smoothly and efficiently across the face of the coal, getting the maximum cut from the least mechanical movement. In Moe's hands, the sixty-ton machine moves with economy and speed in a manner that could almost be described as graceful.

That night, as usual, Moe operated the miner from a remote control box hanging around his neck. He stood about twenty feet behind the machine and just off to the right. Miner operators are required to keep their distance from the machine for their own safety; you never know when the roof is going to collapse or when the cutter head is going to rip into something unexpected—an old well, a shelf of impenetrable rock. Strange things happen in coal mines, and many of them happen in the vicinity of the miner.

That night, however, nothing strange was going on. The crew—Moe was one of nine guys in that section of the mine—had been hitting a lot of water when they drilled support holes in the roof of the mine, but most of the guys saw that as more of a hassle than a danger sign. A lot of mines are wet.

Using a pair of levers on the remote control, Moe sent the miner digging into the coal seam for one last cut before he moved on to another section. Dennis Hall, whom the guys on the crew call Harpo, had just pulled in behind him with a shuttle car—a small underground dump truck—to haul away his last load.

MOE:

Everything was going fine. I was cutting into the face, loading coal. Harpo was right there in his shuttle car. I looked at his car, and I'm thinking I need one more car full; then I'm done with this cut. Then Harpo turned around in his seat, and I looked back at the miner. I did a double take. The front end of the miner is illuminated pretty good, but for some reason I couldn't see the lights on the miner. First I thought I lost power. I looked at the methane monitor in the back and it was still lit up. I looked back at Harpo and looked back at the miner and . . . son of a bitch, holy fuck, what is it? I yelled at Harpo, "Get the fuck out of here now!"

And then I just jumped back into the crosscut, away from a wall of water that was coming at me.

Although Moe didn't realize it at the time, he had just cut into an abandoned mine. And like most old mines, it was flooded with water—a lot of it. Over the years, the water had filled up about seven miles of underground rooms and tunnels; in effect, the old mine had been transformed into an enormous underground lake. When Moe ripped a hole in its wall, seventy million gallons of water suddenly gushed through a six-foot-wide gash. It was like poking a hole in Hoover Dam.

MOE:

I've got eight buddies in this mine with me, I thought, and we're all going to die.

2 · COAL COUNTRY

SOMERSET IS about two hours east of Pittsburgh, in the heart of the southern Pennsylvania coalfields. It's a small town set amid softly rolling hills, with an imposing copper-domed courthouse and streets of tidy brick houses that were built for mine and foundry workers around the turn of the century. It's the kind of town that might have been described as "bustling" fifty years ago, but now feels a little forlorn, and is best known for its craft festivals, for its county fair, and as the crash site of Flight 93, which went down in a field thirteen miles outside of Somerset on September 11, 2001.

The most prominent landmark in town is the Inn at Georgian Place, a restored brick mansion that sits high on a bluff just off the turnpike, surrounded by shuttered factory outlet stores. It is the former home of D. B. Zimmerman, one of the region's most prosperous coal barons, a man who made millions digging this ancient black rock out of the ground and selling it to factories and steel plants. Like many

Industrial Age coal barons, Zimmerman was not exactly beloved by the men who worked for him; in fact, in 1911, an angry employee slashed him with a knife and nearly killed him. The mansion, built in 1915, is a reminder of the tremendous wealth generated by the black rocks that were pulled out of these hills, as well as the enormous gap that has always existed in the coal industry between those who work in the mines and those who own them.

After coal's heyday in the 1920s and 30s, the industry fell on hard times in the 1950s and 60s, when nuclear power and oil seemed to be the energy sources of the future. In Somerset, the mansions were abandoned, jobs were cut, and mines closed down. Coal seemed to be a dying industry, a relic of the Industrial Age, soon to be replaced by cleaner sources of power.

Then, in the 1970s, thanks to the double whammy of the Three Mile Island meltdown and the oil crisis in the Middle East, coal was once again America's fuel source of choice. Overnight, Somerset was jumpin' again. Coal industry executives helicoptered in from Pittsburgh for lunch; Lear jets lined up on the tarmac at the Somerset airport. "Ladies from Pittsburgh would arrive in restaurants wearing furs and diamond tiaras," says Jon Knupp, who was the general manager of the Ramada Inn in Somerset at the time. "You could smell the money."

Of course, the men in the mines didn't share in this

bonanza, but they were making a good living. The mines were mostly unionized, and the coal companies needed every man they could find: If you had a strong back and didn't mind getting dirty, you were hired.

In the 1980s, the party ended. The U.S. steel industry, a large user of coal, shut down numerous plants. The power industry, prompted by new laws that addressed the environmental and public health costs of burning coal, switched to natural gas. The price of coal plummeted, and the fortunes of Somerset sagged. The United States still burns almost a billion tons of coal a year, but most of it comes from big strip mines in West Virginia, Kentucky, and Wyoming.

You can see symbols of the coal industry's decline all over Somerset County. The hills are full of rusting mining equipment and abandoned coal pits, unemployed young men and old men on respirators. In 1907, nearly 352,000 men worked in the Pennsylvania mines. Today there are only about 8,600 in the state. Coal mining—particularly laborious underground coal mining—is, as one of the Quecreek miners put it, a dying beast.

The Quecreek mine, about six miles north of Somerset, is a typical mine for the area—small, tight, and profitable only if everything goes just right. It's operated by Black Wolf Coal Company, which, in a complex financial and legal arrangement common in the industry, is a subsidiary of PBS Coals, Inc., one of the largest coal companies left in the region. The mine opened in early 2001, after the rights to the coal were bought cheap in a tax sale from another mining company.

The sixty or so miners employed at Quecreek were intimately familiar with the coal industry's hard times; all they had to do was look at their paychecks. Most of them were making close to what they had been making a decade earlier. (Like most mines in the area today, Quecreek is nonunion; wages top out at a little over fifteen dollars an hour.) They'd seen mines closed down, their 401(k)s reduced, their health benefits cut. They knew very well they were not working in a boomtown industry anymore; in fact, most of them were grateful to have a job at all.

And like most miners, they bitched and moaned a lot about their greedy bosses, but many of them loved the work itself. It may be hard to understand why any sane person would want to do this for a living. (The industry's safety record has improved in recent years, but coal mining is still among the most dangerous occupations in the United States.) But there's something about working deep in the earth, in the darkness, with death hanging above you in creaking hunks of slate, that's both meaningful and challenging in a way that shuffling pixels on a computer screen can never be. Plus, in an economy like Somerset's, there aren't a whole lot of options: Fifteen dollars an hour in a coal mine beats seven dollars an hour at Wal-Mart.

The crew that headed into the Quecreek mine that July afternoon was a particularly prideful bunch. Led by a forty-four-year-old local boy named Randy Fogle, they were often the top loading crew in the mine, regularly digging out seven hundred or more tons of coal during an eight-hour shift—an impressive rate of production given the conditions and equipment in the mine.

Much of their success and unity, they all admit, was due to Randy's leadership. A third-generation coal miner, Randy has worked in the mines for more than twenty years. He's been both a mine superintendent and a mine supervisor, and has seen it all: cave-ins and collapses, fire and black damp, broken belts and lost miners. He drives his crew hard—he likes to threaten to kill guys if they don't get something done fast enough. But he earns the guys' respect because when the work gets rough—when the roof is starting to sag, or when there is water pouring in and conditions are miserable—he's always there with his men, in the thick of it.

When you meet Randy, his gifts aren't immediately apparent. He's a big, heavy guy with blue eyes and a mustache, and comes off more like a genial uncle than a tough coal miner (if you ignore the big wad of chewing tobacco under his lip). In fact, to see him moving around his living room in his small, nicely kept home in Garrett, where he lives with his wife, Annette, and two of their three kids, he seems like a man ill suited to coal mining. He moves gracelessly, with a noticeable limp.

But underground, Randy is a different person. His eyes spark and jump, his limp disappears, and he moves quickly and smoothly in what coal miners call their duck walk—a hunched-over gait that's almost gorilla-like, using a miner's hammer as a walking stick. Randy gets worked up just looking at the roof (a miner's word for the top, or ceiling, of a coal mine) and ribs (walls) of a mine; he'll talk about the roll and pitch of it for hours. He's so animated, and so knowledgeable and confident, that you instinctively trust him and would follow him anywhere.

Of all the guys on the crew, Randy is probably closest to his fishing buddy, Moe. They have worked together in mines for years, and have spent many hours together casting for pike and bass in nearby lakes. They even took a trip up to northern Ontario recently, flying in on a floatplane to a remote lake known for its awesome pike fishing. Moe's two boys, Daniel, nine, and Lucas, ten, are also passionate fishermen. They live in a clean, simple house overlooking a small lake just outside Somerset. Moe's wife, Sandy, grew up on a lovely farm just down the road, and she still helps milk the cows every day.

There's a lot of overlap between farming and mining in

Somerset. In fact, another member of Randy's crew, John Unger, who has twenty-eight years underground, always dreamed of quitting the mines and running his own dairy farm. At fifty-two, he's a strong, broad-shouldered guy, with a school-of-hard-knocks wisdom that comes from having two kids and a wife who has been diagnosed with multiple sclerosis. Last summer, after being shuffled from lousy mine to lousy mine, Unger threatened to quit and go milk cows. When he finally got a chance to work with Randy, however, he decided to stick around a while longer. "Randy is my main man," says Unger.

The bonds between these guys are often forged by more than just the years they've spent together in the mines. Dennis Hall, forty-nine, knew John Unger from the time he was a little boy, when Unger's father was a greenskeeper at the nearby North Fork Country Club, and they have been friends ever since. Hall—who got tagged with the nickname Harpo because he used to have long blond hair—is a skinny guy with a nervous manner. He too comes from solid coal mining stock: His grandfather started in the mines when he was six years old and worked straight through until he was sixty-two. Harpo has a reputation as a hard worker and a guy who likes his beer and tobacco (he's the only one on the crew who both chews and smokes). For fun, he makes high quality hunting knives, and often arrived at the job with hands nicked from honing the blades.

The only unmarried guy in the bunch was Bob Pugh, who earned the nickname Boogie when his Italian-born grandfather caught him picking his nose when he was a little boy. Boogie was a football and wrestling star in high school. He married the homecoming queen, and they had three kids together before splitting up. At fifty, Boogie still has an athlete's build and gait. He's been dating his girlfriend, Cindy, who owns a beauty salon just down the road, for six years, but he resists marrying or moving in with her, partly because he likes his space. "I tend to spread out in bed like Jesus on the cross," he jokes.

One of Boogie's grade school friends was Ron Hileman, a.k.a. Hound Dog. They've been buddies for forty years now. Hound Dog, forty-nine, describes himself as a laid-back country boy, but you could always count on him to speak his mind when things weren't going well in the mine. His wife, Cathy, runs a day care center out of their home. The kids sometimes called him "sissy," just to tease him.

The scrappiest guy on the crew was Tom Foy, fifty-two. He's a short, tough fireplug of a man, with closely cropped gray hair and a mischievous sparkle in his eye. When he was a kid, someone tagged him Tucker, after the nursery rhyme "Little Tommy Tucker." The fading tattoos on his arms are reminders of his years as a gunner during the Vietnam War. Now he's a doting grandpa.

Tucker also happens to be Blaine Mayhugh's father-in-law. Tucker, in fact, helped Blaine get a job in the mines when his old job spraying lawns was just not paying the bills. At thirty-one, Blaine was the youngest guy in the mine and the one with the least experience underground—only five years. He is also the only one not born into a mining family and the only one over six feet tall. A handsome, buff guy with light blue eyes and high cheekbones, he is a hard worker and a big practical joker, always putting baby powder in someone's helmet or hiding sardine cans in someone's equipment so that it stinks to holy hell.

John Phillippi, thirty-six, was the next to youngest on the crew. He is a solidly built guy with a goatee, heavy eyes, and a gentle smile. He picked up the nickname Flathead somewhere, and was best known on the crew for his amazing ability to nap anytime, anywhere. A few years ago, Flathead and his family had packed up and moved out to Colorado, hoping to make a fresh start. Flathead found a job in a mine, but he hated the remoteness of the place, and they quickly decided they wanted to come back to Somerset County. "Randy made sure I had a job when I got back," Flathead says. "I don't know what I would have done without him."

Quecreek was a fairly standard operation for an underground mine in southwestern Pennsylvania. You enter through a long, low tunnel, about four and a half feet high and twenty feet wide, that has been cut out of a grassy hillside. The floor of the mine gently slopes downward; the air is moist and cool, about 55 degrees year-round. The tunnel quickly opens into a broader area called the main section, or the mains, for short. This is the beginning of the actual working section of the mine.

Quecreek was dug out by a method known as room-and-pillar mining, in which the coal is removed in a series of rooms, or entries, with big blocks of coal left in to keep the roof from collapsing. The mains feel less like a tunnel and more like a big, confusing maze of black rooms. There are seven entries at Quecreek, and each one is numbered from left to right (number one entry is at the far left; number seven, at the far right). Running between each entry, at roughly sixty-foot intervals, are crosscuts, which allow access from one entry to the next.

The roof height in a mine depends on the thickness of the coal seam; the miners literally follow the coal. At Quecreek, where they were cutting a seam called the Upper Kittanning, the roof height varied between four and five feet. Even Tucker, the shortest guy on the crew, had to stoop.

The mains run almost a mile—5,000 feet—into the earth. At the end, a new section juts off to the left—this called, not surprisingly, one left. It's a big, broad corridor virtually identical to the mains, with seven entries and numerous crosscuts between them. It extends back about 3,000 feet. It was here, at the end of one left, about a mile and a half from daylight, that Randy and the others were working.

There were nine guys on the crew that night. At the top, of course, was the foreman, Randy, who was in charge of everything going on underground. His job, to put it simply, was to keep the crew alive and loading as much coal as humanly possible.

Flathead was the official miner operator, in charge of the sixty-ton machine that cuts the coal. Moc was designated as the miner's assistant, although because of his many years of experience, he spent as much time running the miner as Flathead.

Boogie and Harpo were the shuttle car operators, ferrying the coal from the back of the miner to the beltway in speedy little electric dump trucks.

Hound Dog and Unger were bolters. They operated the low, heavy machine that drills holes in the roof and then spins four-foot-long bolts up into it to keep the mine from collapsing while the miners work.

Finally, there's the scoop, which Blaine operated. The scoop is a low, heavy tractor with a big bucket in the front. After the miner leaves an entry, the scoop operator comes in and cleans up any loose coal. He's also in charge of spreading rock dust on the walls to keep the flammable coal dust down so that, in case of a fire, the mine doesn't turn into an underground inferno.

Although all this might sound complex, it really isn't. The miner cuts the coal, the shuttle car driver hauls it away, the bolters secure the roof, the scoop driver cleans up the mess.

Ideally, everyone works together as a team, anticipating one another's actions. When it's going right, it's a symphony of heavy machinery, and for the guys who are part of it, there is even a kind of elegance and beauty to it. In the darkness and noise, you feel deeply connected to your buddies, your machinery, and the earth itself.

Of course when things go wrong, you have another feeling entirely.

3 · A WORLD OF WATER

THAT AFTERNOON, Randy and his crew started arriving at the mine a little after 2 P.M.—Moe in his spotless forest green Toyota Tacoma, Blaine in his slightly beat-up blue Nissan pickup, Boogie in his big red Ford. They headed into what is euphemistically called the locker room—actually, a sagging mobile home outfitted with pegs to hang their clothes and shelves for their boots. Flathead pulled in late as usual—it was a running joke that he was always the last one to arrive.

While they razzed Flathead, they suited up: well-worn long johns, coal-stained blue coveralls, and steel-toed rubber boots. Last to go on were their heavy leather tool belts, which also doubled as dog tags: on each belt, inscribed in a brass plate, are the miner's name and social security number. After a fire or cave-in, at times the brass plate is the only way to identify a body.

When everyone was ready to go, they checked their mining lights, grabbed their battered helmets, mining hammers, and self-rescuers—an awkward canteen-like piece of equipment that in an emergency gives them air to breathe for an hour—and headed down to the pit.

BOOGIE:

We drive into the mine on a flat little cart called a mantrip. It takes about a half hour to get from the pit, where the entrance is, to the face, where we're cutting.

We talk about all kinds of stuff while we're heading down. Sometimes, if it's early in the morning, some of the guys sleep.

That day, when we started in on the mantrip, John Unger looked at me and said, "Hey, Boog, loan me about forty thousand bucks." I said, "What do you mean, John?" He said, "Me and my partner want to get twenty-five head of cattle from Canada, heifers already bred. We're kicking it around and we're going to bring them back here and we're going to sell them and make, like, two hundred apiece on these cows."

I said, "Forty thousand—yeah, right, you're crazy, man." They figured I'm single, I've got all the money.

Well, we're kicking it around, teasing him a little. Unger is a semiprofessional farmer and we tease him about farming like we know more than him. And we piss him off. "I gotta go home and do the back forty," I say. Or "Hey, John, I baled some hay last night."

But Unger gives it back too. I told him one time, "Yeah, I was hunting, and I had to cross this bob wire . . ." "Hold on, wait a minute," he said. "What did you call it?" I said, "Bob wire." He said, "It's *barbed* wire, it ain't bob wire." And then he started teasing me about bob wire. He thought that was hilarious.

BLAINE:

We always sang "Green Acres" to John. Or we teased him about his tongue. He has a huge tongue. We were always saying, "Let me see your tongue, John!" I liked to tell him that if he put some leather pants on and stuck out his tongue and let us take a picture of him, we could set up a site on the Internet and make a fortune.

FLATHEAD:

I was running the miner the first part of the shift. Moe and I, we're both miner operators, and we trade off. I usually take the first part of the shift, he takes the second. At eight o'clock, I said, "I'm going to eat, it's my time." And I went back behind the miner and sat down and ate my lunch. I had kipper steaks—sardines.

As they cut into the coal face, most of the men were aware that 300 feet or so ahead of them lay the old Saxman mine. The Saxman mine had been opened in 1923, and before it closed forty years later, almost four million tons of coal had been removed from it. There was nothing unusual about operating in the vicinity of a closed-up mine. After all, Pennsylvania is full of old mines. That's one reason why every new mine has to be precisely surveyed, and why state and federal mining laws require mine operators to keep 200 feet away from any old workings. And according to the map at Quecreek, the area they were working in was still well beyond the buffer zone.

But of course no map is perfect. Every miner has stories about hitting old tunnels and other unexpected surprises underground. Often it's no big deal; sometimes it's a nightmare. In 1959, miners working underground near Pittston, Pennsylvania, accidentally cut into the Susquehanna River. The river flooded the mine, killing twelve men and causing such an enormous whirlpool in the river that engineers eventually drove train cars into the water in a desperate attempt to plug the hole.

JOHN UNGER:

I don't care what the maps said, I didn't like the roof. About a week earlier, I told Randy, "It's really changing in here. Whatever's up in front of us, it's big." I told him we're really going to run into some bad stuff here eventually. I think how I explained it was "This place is going to turn ugly shortly."

On that particular day, I was really having a tough time. It was the water, mostly—we were hitting buckets of it. And I mean buckets. Hound Dog and I run the bolter. We drill holes in the roof of the mine, then throw 42-inch bolts up there and tighten them up. The bolts support the roof, keep it from collapsing while you're working.

That day Hound Dog was killing me, man. He was dry. I was wet. That's the way it works sometimes—one side would be wet and one side would be dry. And I was taking a beating. We'd only been in there a few hours, and I was soaked already.

I said, "Let's just finish it up and go home. I'm sick of this."

MOE:

In a mine, conditions control everything—whether it's wet, high, low, dry, whatever. When the mine is fairly high and fairly dry and there's a good roof, I mean, that's super. But this mine at Quecreek was pretty low, about four foot where we was working, and it was wet. We were down on our hands and knees, you know; it was cold and wet and dark. It was a real swamp hole.

The bolters, Hound Dog and Unger, get the worst of it. I was feeling bad for them.

HOUND DOG:

I was teasing John: "Hey, gettin' a little wet?" Every time he'd drill into the roof, water would pour out.

Before, we'd hit maybe one hole of full pipe before this and maybe another hole. And then it would dry up for a little bit and then you'd hit more water. But this was continuous—every hole.

It's not unusual to hit water in a mine. The earth is full of holes, cracks, fissures—all of which contain pockets of water. Usually it runs off quickly and is gone in five minutes.

When you're hitting this much water, however, it slows everything up, and the whole rhythm of the mine is disrupted.

FLATHEAD:

If we load over a certain number of tons of coal a month, we get a bonus. One month we got an extra five hundred dollars. So, you know, we were shooting for that again. And the water was really slowing us up.

UNGER:

We wanted to move to another part of the mine where it was drier and we could load more coal. But the bosses said, "Well, you've got one more crosscut to finish up."

The swamp hole turned into a hellhole the moment Moe cut into the old mine. Harpo was only about fifteen feet behind him, waiting in his shuttle car.

HARPO:

I was loaded, already turned around in my seat and ready to go. Moe was finishing loading me. Next thing I know, Moe hollers at me. Well, I took off. I felt the water hit me in the back.

I didn't know where Moe went, if he had been washed away or what.

HOUND DOG:

I was working a couple entries over, in entry four. All of a sudden, the power on the bolter kicks. So that's nothing abnormal. We're standing around there waiting. Usually somebody will just run down and reset it. Within five minutes or so, your lights come back on your machine, you're ready to go. So we didn't go anywhere. We're just standing there—no, not standing there, the mine is too low. You're kneeling—kneeling, waiting for the power to come back on.

It might have went two minutes, three minutes, I don't know exactly. Here comes Tucker running across the entry saying, "We cut into some old workings. Get out!" I looked over and I seen some water running down but it didn't look real, real bad.

BLAINE:

I heard a noise, a roar. I wasn't even thinking of the water that much; I was thinking gas. I was just thinking maybe black damp or methane. I was afraid there was an explosion.

UNGER:

Water and fire are the two worst things to deal with in there. I mean, you can handle rock falls, roof falls, and things like that. But water and fire are the worst. You get water and fire, you got big-time trouble, big-time.

RANDY:

When I heard that water, I thought to myself, This ain't good, because I knowed what was ahead of us. I knowed there was a mine up there and we was supposed to be, like, three hundred feet from it. I said, "I know what we hit." And I told Tom, "Get everybody together in the feeder [where the coal is loaded onto the belt-way]." I told Harpo, "Get to the phone and tell every-body to get out."

As Randy knew very well, there were nine guys working in another section of the mine. Because that section was lower than where Randy's crew was working, the water would head down to them first. And unless someone gave them a heads-up, they'd never know what was coming until it was too late.

HARPO:

The phone is right there on the wall, a couple hundred feet from where I was standing. The phone just goes outside and to where the other crew is working. I pick it up and I'm yelling for the guys in the mains. "Hey, mains! Hey, mains! Mains! Mains! Anybody in the mains? Anybody in the mains? Hey, mains! Hey, mains!" I got desperate. I couldn't raise the mains. I'm still, "Hey, mains! Mains! Mains!" Decided to call outside: "Outside, outside, outside! Outside, outside, outside, outside, outside!" I get ahold of somebody. He answers. "Hey, we got major water coming in this place! You got to try to get ahold of the mains!" And just about that time somebody from the mains answers. "Hey, you guys, we got major water coming in this fucking place, get the fuck out, and I mean get the fuck out now, and I mean fucking *now*, out!"

The guys in the mains got the message—they immediately dropped their tools and ran. Within a few minutes, they were swamped by a mean torrent of waist-high water. But because of their advance warning, they were able to fight their way out of the mine. As Doug Custer, one of the nine miners who escaped, later put it: "Without that phone call, we would have been dead."

HOUND DOG:

At first I didn't understand the magnitude of the situation we were in. Remember, there's a lot of mined-out coal below us. I mean, that probably could have held a couple of thousand gallons of water. I figured the way the mines laid, you'd have to go down the belt three thousand feet and make it around the belt head and then go through a big dip. And then it's pretty much uphill to the outside. I wasn't too much concerned right at that time. I was more concerned about the long walk out that was ahead of me.

We was calm. Our backs was hurting. We're not used to walking around in there. When you work in the mines, you go to your machine and you're on your knees. You move around from entry to entry to bolt or mine or whatever, but you're still not walking along much.

We even sat down and took a little break there.

TUCKER:

This mine we're working in, it's a big mine. In order for that water to get clear up to where we were, it had to fill up lots of rooms, some places about as high as ten, twelve feet. So we figured, my goodness, we have all kinds of time.

The only guy who was clearly in desperate straits was Moe. After jumping out of the way of the sudden blast of water, he found himself trapped in a narrow area between the raging water and the outer wall of the mine.

MOE:

The bulk of the water is coming straight back through the number six entry. But it's bleeding down through all these crosscuts, and it's bouncing off the ribs. At this time, I'm in water roughly up to my balls.

At one point, I looked across and saw lights. I knew they were looking for me. But I knew what the situation was. I knew this mine is filling up really, really fast. We had very little time.

I just sorta waved them off with my light. I was more worried about them guys. They got to get the hell out, you know. Don't piss around waiting for me.

RANDY:

I went over to see where Moe was at because he was the operator, and I didn't know what happened to him. When I got there, I found him standing there on the other side of this raging river of water, sort of trapped between the water and a wall of coal. The noise was so loud right there it was like a jet engine—you could scream at the top of your lungs, but you couldn't hear nothing. I tried to tell him to work his way down the intake, and then I'd try to pick him up down there if we could get a place that slowed down, but I don't think he heard me.

I mean, we both knowed there was no chance that I could get him with me, and there was nothing else we could do. This water was hitting the corner of the ribs and was coming back around just like a big wave. There was no way.

And Moe—he knew what was going on. I locked eyes with him. He shook his head. "Go without me," he was saying. And I went.

That's one of the hardest things I ever did in my life.

MOE:

I watched Randy go. That light disappeared, and I was alone. There was nowhere I could go. The water in front of me—it's like a raging Colorado River. Just gushing. I can't breathe. I'm getting no oxygen. It's taking my oxygen. So I'm gasping. Plus you're shook up, excited. So I'm thinking, I got to calm down. I kept saying, "Please, God. Please, God. Please, God." I can't think of a prayer. I'm not praying, I'm just saying, "Please, God, help me." I'm saying this out loud, you know, so He could hear me.

4 · GOING UNDERGROUND

MOE:

My dad started in the mines when he was thirteen. That's all he ever done. They worked in their own coal mine. It's in our blood, you know. My father's father owned his own mine for a while. He graduated from Carnegie Mellon. There was only, like, fourteen of them that ever graduated from there with a miner degree. He was one of them.

And my father, he was in the mine when the Johnstown Flood hit in 1977, and he come out of the mine hand over hand on a high voltage cable. The water was up to their necks and it was pouring in the mine. I remember him telling me a Doberman pinscher was dead, got its legs on each side of his chest, and he had to pull it off. My dad had about forty-three years in the mines, and he seen an awful lot.

I remember when I was younger, about ten years old, me and him went to a hunting camp we have up north. I didn't understand what went on, but I remember Dad crying at night, and I didn't know why. I found out later that his helper got killed. That's why they gave him time off, to get away, you know.

He was crushed; a roof fell. When I got older, Dad told me what he went through, crawling on top of rocks looking for his helper, trying to see a light, so you can imagine what that did to him. And he lost a lot of friends, guys who worked beside him. This guy was his helper for twelve years. My dad spent more time with him than he did with his family.

First time I went into a mine, I was five years old. Don't remember much, except that it was dark. When we filled out a thing in high school, "What do you want to do after you graduate?" I wrote down: "I want to be a coal miner." How stupid is that?

My dad got me the job. As a matter of fact, my dad ran the miner, and he told the owners that if they didn't give me a job quick, he would slow them down. He said, "You're going to get less coal until you get my boy on."

UNGER:

I grew up on a farm, and it was hard work. I figured I'd try something else for a while. So after I graduated from high school—I was a rowdy kid—I had various jobs, and ended up working as the assistant produce manager at a grocery store. It was a fine job, but it was giving me an ulcer. And I wasn't making any money. By that time I was married to Sue, and we had a child on the way. The best-paying job I could find was in the mines. And I thought, Hell, why not? I'll just do it for a little while, then quit.

Well, the first time I went in, it was kind of exciting because you never see anything like it. You looked at it and you thought, Well, no real big deal. This don't look that bad.

The roof was high when we went in so they could haul supplies in and out. It was about five or six feet. I thought, Well, this is nothing, but then we went up into the face, the actual working section, it was twenty-eight inches high. I'm looking at this and I'm thinking, Holy cow, this is bad. I thought, Well, hey, I'll try it. If I can do it, I can do it. If I can't, I can't. I have to do something, and this pays fifty dollars a day.

So I worked there a couple days and there was this guy, he was the foreman. Oh, he just cursed and swore all the time and he called me Walt instead of my name, John. Every day he called me Walt. I said, "Who are you talking to?" He said, "You, Walt."

I worked with a bunch of experienced guys. I mean to tell you, you talk about taking a beating.

They were on you every day. I mean every day, man, they were screaming at you; whatever you did was wrong. It didn't matter if it was right, it was wrong. I just made up my mind I could do this. I could really, really do this.

And I started there in December of 1974 and I told my wife, "As soon as I get enough money to build a house, I'll quit." I had to have, I think, $5,500 for the down payment. So I worked a bunch of overtime. I bought a new rifle, because I wanted to buy a good gun—a Remington 270. And then the rest of it I saved for the house. But I had to have $5,500. And then things were moving right along there and I didn't quite have enough, so her grandfather loaned me the money to finish what I needed to do so we could get a house, because he wanted us to have our own place.

So we built a house in 1976, and things were going pretty good—bought some cars, stuff like that.

Even though I said I was going to quit, I never did. Then I got the chance to buy my farm in 1980—it was a place I'd always dreamed of owning since I was a kid. Eighty-four acres. Bought some cows. And then we thought about farming and I wanted to milk cows. I figured farming was a better life, after all. I was still working in the mine and I enjoyed it, you know. I don't think I could've just went if it was just a paycheck. It was something I really felt good at. But I always, in the back of my mind—I always wanted to get out, but I never did because I knew I couldn't make a living farming.

BLAINE:

I'm not from a coal mining family. My father worked in construction. I was born in Baltimore, but moved to Somerset County when I was seven. I was a wild boy. I didn't get into a lot of trouble, but I was ornery. I spent a lot of time in the woods up behind our house, making beer and tracking animals and playing poker with my friends. I played a lot of baseball. In high school, I had an 80 m.p.h. fastball and a breaking ball that dropped like two foot.

After high school, I enlisted in the Navy. Spent nine months at sea during Desert Storm on the USS *Seattle*, a combat support ship. I was a petty officer third class. I thought about going for the SEALs, but that didn't work out.

When I was discharged, I went to work for a company in Meyersdale making tabletops. Then I did construction for a while, but that didn't pay nothin', and I had no insurance. By that time Leslie and I was married, and she was in nursing school.

I worked for a company called ChemLawn for about

three years. I enjoyed that, driving around, spraying people's lawns and whatever. But it was only $8.10 an hour, and I was laid off most of the winter.

When my kids were born, I wanted my wife to quit working so many hours—she works at a nursing home here in town—and spend more time with them. My father-in-law, Tom, said he could get me on in the mines. I'd been trying for years, but no luck. But Tom helped me out. That was about five years ago.

I'm a big guy for the mines—I'm six foot. So I had to stoop a lot and was down on my hands and knees. And that first month I started, my whole body ached and burned.

But I didn't really mind the work, you know. And I liked having health insurance, and I liked the bonuses we got for loading extra coal. But it takes its toll on your body. I had to have a cortisone shot a few months ago, my arm was hurting me so bad from running the controls on the scoop all day long. I couldn't even throw a baseball with my son, it was hurting so bad.

RANDY:

My grandfather and his brothers had a mine. It's been in my family for a lot of years. It's got to be in your blood. If it ain't, you might as well forget it. I don't do it for money. Everybody has got to live, and you do it to support your family and that kind of stuff, but it has to be something else.

After high school, I worked on a farm for a while, but then I went to a strip mine. A short time later, I went underground. I didn't have no kids or nothing, and the money at the mine was much better.

Annette, my wife, tried to talk me out of it. Her grandfather had died in the mines when her grandmother was pregnant with her father. But I told her that mines these days are much safer than they used to be.

The first mine I worked at was rough. It was wet, there was a lot of bedrock in it. The first month or two I was there, we had a cave-in and buried some machinery. The roof was real bad, lots of water coming out of it. I almost got killed working there. Big rock fell out of the roof and I got slammed. I was dazed—I didn't even know where I was at. I went right back to work. I had nightmares about it later.

I liked being underground. In all these years, I never broke nothing, never cut nothing off.

For me, there's a lot of pride that goes with working in the mines. I mean, it's something you do well. You don't want to ever say you play a game with this, because coal mining is serious business. It's Mother Nature you're messing with, and it's you and her. That's one of the challenges. You're playing against a force that is awesome. You can never control it because it's bigger than you are. I mean, she's wicked.

5 · BATTLE ON THE BELTWAY

AFTER THE WATER broke through, Flathead was the first guy to head down the beltway, with Blaine following close behind. It is no coincidence that the two youngest men on the crew, both with young children, were also the two men most desperate to get out.

FLATHEAD:

As I headed out, there was not much water in the beltway at first. It was all rushing down the entry beside us. I thought we still had time. But as we got further down, we started wading through water, oh, chest-high, and it was moving fast.

I jumped on the belt and started going down that way, but that was too slow for me because I was so wound up—I wanted to get the hell out of there. So I jumped back into the water and held on to the belt and just waded through it as fast as I could.

BLAINE:

I was like a hundred feet or so behind Flathead. I knew we didn't have much time, we had to get to the mains before the water closed it off. I wasn't thinkin' about nothin' but getting out of there.

A couple of times during this, I lost my helmet—it was so tight in there, it'd bump the roof or whatever, and it fell into the water. If I'd have lost that, I'd have been in trouble. It was the only light I had. I'm, like, "Please, no, don't let my light go out."

HOUND DOG:

I was holding on to the belt structure going down through there. The water was really swift—it almost knocked me off my feet. And it was getting higher and higher as we went down through. And I couldn't keep on my feet no more. A couple times I slipped and I did go under.

Eventually I climbed up on top of the belt and started crawling. The water was up to the top of the belt. I could see the other guys' lights out ahead. They were crawling on the belt ahead of us. There was still guys behind us coming, too—Harpo and Randy Fogle and I don't know who else for sure. There were places where the mine dipped down and the belt got fairly close to the roof. You had to get off your hands and knees and actually lay flat and just shimmy through because the belt was that close to the roof.

But as you're crawling down through there, the water is raging down. It's hitting the belt, splashing up on you; you're breathing it, choking, coughing. It was brown water, I don't know why, but it was brown, and it was rising fast.

RANDY:

After I left Moe, I was the last one to head down the beltway. I had to do some hustling to catch up with the other guys. And that's when I started to feel my heart pounding. It was hard work, fighting that water. I mean, it was as high as our belt, and you're stooped over, and you're trying to run, and the air is getting bad. I decided the best way was to just float along with it. I could hang on the side of the rail and just let it take me down.

HARPO:

At one point, I look back, I see a light. I hollered, "Who is that?" Randy says, "It's me, Randy." "Come on, Randy, let's go! Hurry up! Come on!" I wait for him. He gets close enough to me, I see he's all right, we moved on. The water is trying to take me. I'm hanging on to the belt structure. The water is just trying to take my feet out from under me. I holler back at Randy, "Randy, I'm not going to make it. I ain't going to make it." Then I feel this hand behind me. Randy grabs me by the back of my coveralls and literally throws me up onto the belt. Saved my life.

FLATHEAD:

There is one low spot in the mine, a place where the coal seam just kinda dipped, and when I hit that section, suddenly the water was completely up to the roof.

There was no way that I would even think about trying to swim through it because the current was so fast and you don't know how far you would have had to swim or what you would get into on the other side.

I was really getting scared now. I just yelled back to Blaine, "Turn around, we can't go no more!"

I heard Blaine yell, "You sure, you sure?" And I said, "No, we can't make it." And he said, "Well, what are we going to do?" I said, "We're going to have to go back."

BLAINE:

I didn't want to turn around, but we had no choice. We had been traveling with the water going down. Now we had to fight it back up. And it was still rising. As we was coming back, we all got bunched up and my father-in-law looked at me with the most serious eyes. I mean, you could just see it in his face, he was scared to death. He said, "We're in trouble."

BOOGIE:

I seen Tucker was ahead of me. And he said, "We've got to turn around. We can't go this way." Oh, shit. That's the first time I knowed we may be trapped. We've got to go back. So these guys start coming back. And we're all on the belt trying to crawl like army men.

I had blood flying from my knuckles. I remember the blood coming from holding my hammer, grasping it, and hitting the coal as I was coming up the belt line.

I was afraid the belt line was going to flip over and we were all going to drown.

HOUND DOG:

Going back up that beltway was just like trying to run upstream in a river. You're fighting it all the way. The muscles in your legs and everything is so tense. I mean, you know, all it took was one slip. That water was raging wild. One slip and it would have took you off your feet and you'd have been gone.

BLAINE:

To be honest with you, at one time when I was along the belt there, I was tired and beat up, and for just that split second, I said, "Blaine, let's just let go. Let it take you." It would have been so easy. I ain't lying, my arms—I could barely lift them up. I mean, it was like Jell-O and I'm pulling all I have to get through.

At this moment, it was all fatigue, it wasn't fear. But then I got mad at myself. I said, "Goddamn it, I'm not going to die!" I told myself, "Pull it together—you got a wife, you got kids. There's still a chance."

Eventually all the guys made it back up the beltway far enough so that they were more or less out of the water. They were exhausted but safe.

HOUND DOG:

As soon as we got off the belt, Randy wondered if Moe had gotten out. I said, "I don't know, I haven't seen him." And Unger said the same. Now, I don't know if he got in contact with these other guys that was ahead of us going down the belt, if he had talked to them or not. But I know he asked me, "Do you know where Moe is?" I said, "No, I didn't see him." He said, "Boy, I hope he's all right." I said, "Well, maybe he's ahead of us." John said, "I don't know where he is either."

With the beltway flooded, their only chance now was to try to go out the air return—the partially walled-off passage where the circulating air returns from the mine to outside. "I told them we had to try it," Randy says. "What else were we going to do?"

Initially they didn't hit much water. They could hear it rushing all around them, but the return itself was protected by the walls and was drier than the beltway. As they traveled farther down, the water had blown some doors open, and the water started to rise to their waists. Finally, after scrambling about a thousand feet down the entry, they reached a concrete block wall that cut directly in front of them. On the other side of that wall was the mains—and possibly a way out.

RANDY:

I started beating on the block and it just wore me out, and they yelled at Flathead and he jumped in and started and then somebody else started beating on the wall. And then finally I got a little bit of one block out and—boom!—the water was over our heads right now. It was just the pressure from that side to this side changed and it just . . . it just buried us.

HOUND DOG:

I asked Randy what we were going to do, and he just said, "The water's got us. We're not getting out of here." I mean, everybody knew it. There was no other way out.

6 · THE CALL

——————

ANNETTE FOGLE is a big reader. The modest house she shares with Randy and their kids Brittany, fifteen, and Steven, twenty (their son Matthew, twenty-one, lives on his own), is stuffed with books—*Lonesome Dove, Beach Music,* and lots of Tom Clancy (Randy's favorite). In fact, if you didn't know better, you might mistake her for the local librarian. She's forty, calm and thoughtful, with short brown hair and glasses.

Annette knows mines as well as she knows books. Her grandfather was crushed to death in one in 1938, just as her grandmother was about to give birth to her father. Because of that, her father never worked in the mines—he drove a tar truck. She remembers a nursery rhyme her grandmother taught her when she was a little girl:

My sweetheart's a mule in the mine.
I drive him all day without lines.
On the bumper I sit

While tobacco I spit
All over my sweetheart's behind.

She first met Randy when he was working on the farm where she lived. He was setting fence posts. Her mom looked out at him and said, "There would be a good man for you." Annette was fourteen years old at the time; Randy was eighteen. She wasn't allowed to date until she was sixteen. But after that, they didn't waste any time: They got married when she was seventeen, two weeks after she graduated from high school.

ANNETTE FOGLE:

Randy and I had a fight that morning. I won't talk about it. But he gave me a kiss before he went to work and told me he loved me. I didn't tell him that I loved him, something I regretted later on. He turned and looked at me before he walked out the door. And it was a look that I carried with me for the next couple of days, because it was a strange look.

That night I was doing something that . . . well, in retrospect, it's an odd coincidence. I was in the dining room, using the computer. I was online, playing a game called Noah's Ark. It's a game where you have to put animals two by two into the ark before the floodwaters come up. If the waters get too high and the boat is about to float away, there's a red thing that flashes and warns you that the floodwaters are coming.

It was five after eleven when the phone rang. It was just Brittany and me here at the house. My son Steve wasn't home yet. And if the phone here rings after eleven, I think, well, it's either Steven or there could be some kind of problem—you know, somebody sick.

Brittany answered the phone. She said, "Mom, it's for you." And I asked her who it was, and she said, "It's a salesman." I thought, Five after eleven, it's a salesman? So I got on the phone and this state trooper introduced himself. I almost said, "Well, what did Steven do now?"

He said that there had been an accident at the mine and that there was some men unaccounted for. And they wanted the families to come to Sipesville, to the fire hall, if they wanted to. He couldn't tell me any details.

From there, my mind was a blank. I don't remember a thing he said after that.

Missy Phillippi, thirty-four, has a tattoo of a vine wrapped around her left ankle. She's blond, outspoken, and tough as Pennsylvania steel—you don't mess with Missy. She and John (Flathead) live in a small barn-shaped house with their twelve-year-old son Christopher. Talking to Missy, you get the feeling she knows what it's like to lose the things you love, and she's fiercely protective of her husband and family life.

Like Annette, Missy was sitting at her computer, going online, when the call came from the state police.

MISSY PHILLIPPI:

When I called the mine, Dave, the mine clerk, picked up the phone. I know Dave—I could hear his voice shaking. I said, "This is Melissa Phillippi. I was told to call the mine, there was an incident." He said, "Yes, ma'am. There's been an accident, you're to go to Sipesville fire hall, and they'll give you more details there." I said, "Wait a minute. An accident—what do you mean? Was there a cave-in?" "No, ma'am," he said. So I said, "Are they trapped?" "Yes, ma'am." And I said, "Is it bad? You have to tell me." He said, "Yes, ma'am, it's bad."

I said, "Is John in there?" and he said, "Yes, ma'am, we think so." And about that time I looked over and my twelve-year-old son Chris was standing in the hallway. And Chris goes, "Mom, what is going on?" And I'm, like, "I don't know, Chris. Something happened at the mine. Your dad is trapped."

John Unger swears he knew he wanted to marry Sue as soon as he set eyes on her in the first grade. "It was her long pigtails," John says. "I think I was in love with her from the get-go." You can see why: She's a small but forceful woman, with short dark hair and large dark eyes that radiate inner strength and good humor. She was diagnosed with multiple sclerosis in 1987, and although she must use a walker to get around, she remains determinedly independent, driving herself around town and back and forth from her job at a local church. She and John have two kids, Stephen and Vicki.

SUE UNGER:

About 11 P.M. that night, I was pretty tired. I decided to take a shower. I went into the bathroom and the news was on. And I thought I heard them say something about the company that runs the Quecreek mine—Black Wolf. And I thought, Nah, I'm hearing things. And the last part was miners trapped. And again I thought, Nah.

When I got out of the bathroom, there was a message on the machine from the state police, asking me to call the mine. I had to look the number up in the book. When I reached them, they told me that John was trapped. I said, "By himself or with other people?" They said, "No, the whole crew is there." They told me to go to the Sipesville firehouse, where they'd keep me informed about what was going on.

So I got myself ready, and I drove down there. When

I arrived, I didn't know how to get into the building. There was no handicapped entrance that I could see. So I stood outside. All the windows were open, and I could hear them talking in there. So I just stood there and listened for a while. Then one of the chaplains who was there came out and wanted to know if I wanted to come in. I said, "Yes, if there is a way I could get in." He goes, "Walk the whole way around and you can get in the back." So I went in. And I sat there all night waiting.

One of the miners who had been on the other crew, the crew that escaped, was there, answering phones and trying to keep us updated. His name was Doug Custer. I felt so bad for him. I could see him when he'd answer the phone, and just by the look on his face, I was trying to decide if it was good news or bad news. There was only one time I really thought it was bad because his face just dropped and he was running his hands through his hair. And I thought, Oh, this is it.

But I think now it was just that he was so overwhelmed because there was nothing he could really tell us. He just hung up the phone and said, "The situation is still the same." They really don't know where they are or what's really going on. At that point, they didn't even know if they were alive. But then I thought, Well, maybe I shouldn't watch his face anymore when he answers the phone.

Leslie Mayhugh was the only family member in double jeopardy during all this: Both her husband, Blaine, and her father, Tom Foy (Tucker), were working in the mine that day. "I had everything at stake," Leslie says. "My past and my future."

She and Blaine live in a small house in Meyersdale, twenty miles from the mine. It's just down the street from the house Blaine grew up in, and where his parents still live. Leslie, a bright-eyed, animated woman who loves to blast heavy metal rock—Def Leppard, Metallica—around the house, works every other weekend as a licensed practical nurse at a local nursing home. She and Blaine have two kids, Kelsey, seven, and Tyler, eight.

LESLIE MAYHUGH:

When I got to the firehouse all I knew was that there had been a mine accident and water was coming in and it's a lot of water. But there is some good news—half the guys got out. And I said, "Half of them got out?" I realized he was talking about the guys in the other part of the mine. But I still wasn't sure if Blaine and my father were down there.

Finally, when Dave Rebuck, the contractor who was running the mine, came in, he just said some of them got out and some didn't. I was, like, "Just tell me, I want to know. Are Blaine and my dad in there?" But he wouldn't say. He just put his head down and walked by me. I was right at the door because we needed fresh air. I said to my mom, "I want to ask him, I have to know, I can't take this uncertainty."

So I went up to him—I was pretty upset—and I said, "Are my dad and Blaine down there?" I wanted an answer. And he couldn't tell me yes. But he nodded his head. Of course I lost it and I went in and told my mom, "It's them." At least I knew. Because otherwise I would have spent the whole night looking out at this hillside, waiting for Blaine to come walking, muddy, wet, right up to me.

7 · RESCUING MOE

MOE:

I don't know how long I was there after I saw those guys leave. Few hours. I lost track. I figured they was gone, they got out. If I was going to get out, I had to do it on my own.

I was stuck in a very small area, maybe twenty feet wide and seventy feet long. The water was still raging beside me, and I had a wall of coal on the other. After looking around, I noticed there was a golf cart partly underwater just below me. It had some stuff on it—electrical tape, a raincoat, a toolbox.

I put the raincoat on right away because it was starting to get cold. Breathing was a big factor. I'd keep trying to calm myself down. Well, I knew it was lack of oxygen. And I was thinking, Please, God. I was looking for help all the time, you know, thinking of my kids, got to get out of here, got to get across this water. How do I get across this water?

I went to see if the golf cart would run. Well, I wasn't going to go nowhere, but I just wanted to see if it would move. I turned the light on, pointed it toward that hole in the wall, thinking if they do come back up, maybe they'll see it.

I made camp at that golf cart. I thought, This is where it's going to happen. I got to come up with a plan. I'm looking around. There's very little options—no options.

After failing to escape out the return, Randy and the others were slowly working their way back up toward the face, where it was still high and dry. The air was getting bad; it smelled of sulfur. Several of the older guys, including Tucker and Randy, were having a tough time. About four hours had passed since Moe first broke into the old mine. Now, after fighting the water for most of that time, they were all exhausted and depressed.

About the only thing keeping them going was Moe— they wanted to find him. Blaine and Tucker went ahead and started pushing open the small doors that separated the intake from the main section of the mine, hoping they might find some trace of him. Flathead went back up toward the phone, hoping he might be able to call out, but the water had washed away the line.

Meanwhile, Moe, thinking the other guys were either gone or dead, hatched his escape plan.

MOE:

I'm looking for ways across this river. There's no way I can do it, but I have to. I have to save myself. I have to try.

So I'm looking around. I see the water hose coming through. I thought about tying that to my waist and trying to walk across, but no, that ain't going to work. I see hydraulic hoses on that golf cart, a four-foot hose. I thought I'd wrap that around me, then tape it to the water line and try to go across this way.

So I tie this hose around me, then I tape it to the water line really tight. I mean, I just tape the shit out of it. I figure, hell, I better tape my hard hat on, too. If I lost my hat and my light, I'd be screwed.

I step out into the water. I think, No way, this ain't going to work neither. I had to find some way to pull me across here, so I'm thinking, thinking, thinking. There's J-hooks strung across the roof above the water. We used them for hanging cables out of the way. Can't reach them. So I use some tools that was in the toolbox. I tape them all together and make a pole. I fish them off the roof and tape them to my hands, so I had like hooks on my hands.

My idea was that I was going to use these J-hooks to hook onto the roof and kinda climb across. Like monkey bars, you know.

I get my other stuff ready. I find a hammer that is on the golf cart because my hammer is gone. I keep the raincoat on. I thought I might need the hammer because if I cross this water, I got to knock that wall out to get through it, so I have this ball-peen hammer. I tape it to my belt so I don't lose it in the water.

Finally, I say, "Well, hell, I got to get moving. I got to try it." I figured I could go backward on my back so the water would keep me afloat because it was going that fast.

I'm two steps into the water. It is probably three feet deep, but it's running ninety miles an hour. It's just flying up and hitting me. The third step, I keep putting my foot in, but it is so deep and fast, it just keeps taking my foot away. I had it in my mind I ain't going to make it. But I had to try something. If I was going to die, I at least wanted to die trying to get out, rather than just sitting there waiting to drown or suffocate.

So I'm getting ready to turn around there and throw myself in and I see a light.

FLATHEAD:

I walked up a little bit past the feeder and I had seen the golf-cart light on the other side of the water. There was a little hole in one of the walls, letting some of the light through, so I went over and knocked some more block out and there was Moe.

MOE:

When I saw that light, I jumped right back to dry land. I looked over and I seen it was Flathead. I yelled, "Man, am I glad to see you, buddy!"

Flathead signaled to Moe that he was going to get the other guys, then ran back to tell them what he'd found. "Man, did that lift our spirits," says Tucker. They all hustled over and stood at the edge of the gushing water across from Moe. It was only about twenty feet, but with the torrent of water, it may as well have been a mile. How were they going to get him across?

HOUND DOG:

When we all went up there, that was the first time we got to see the water up close, to really understand what was coming in. Just a wild, rushing river. I mean, just the wildest rushing river that you can imagine.

RANDY:

Flathead said, "You better talk to Moe, he ain't taking it too good." Moe was in tough shape. I mean, he's hyperventilating, froze to death, scared to death, by himself. I mean, that's pretty rough. When I got over there, he said, "I got to get out of here, Randy." "You will," I told him. But I wasn't sure how.

First they tried throwing a long piece of cable across, hoping Moe could grab it and they could pull him through the water. No way. The water just washed the cable away before Moe could grab it. They tried reaching across with a bolter probe—a twenty-foot-long metal rod—but it was too flimsy.

Randy wondered if they could just wait for the old mine to empty itself, or at least slow down so Moe could get across. But that could take hours, and the water showed no signs of running itself out.

Finally Randy came up with a last-ditch plan: He'd drive the scoop into the raging water, and hopefully the bucket would reach far enough across so that Moe could jump into it. It was an outlandish idea: What if the water swept the scoop down the entry? After all, it had already pushed the sixty-ton miner twenty feet back. Whoever was driving the scoop would probably go down with it. And what if Moe missed the bucket when he jumped?

RANDY:

When I explained to Tucker what I was going to do, he said, "Well, there ain't no way you're going to get over there with that. It's just going to take it down." I said, "Well, I got to try. Moe ain't going to stay over there much longer."

BLAINE:

Because it was my scoop, I thought I was going to drive it. I would have given it a try. But Randy said, "I'll do it." And my father-in-law took me aside and said, "You're not doing it, Blaine."

UNGER:

I said to Randy, "Man, there's nothing I can do to help you if that thing starts to go. If you get out in there, we'll sit and watch you go by." So I told him, "All you need to do is just inch it out and inch it out. It's really easy as long as you keep back where it's fairly anchored." I said, "You might be able to back away from it if it does get carried away."

RANDY:

I just took it tentatively. As I inched the scoop out into the water, I had the tires up against the rib of the mine, hoping that would help hold it. I felt it around a little bit, you know, and I got to a point I couldn't go much farther. I yelled at Moe, "Far enough?" He shook his head no. I thought, Oh, boy, this is getting pretty touchy here. So I wiggled around a couple more feet and I yelled, "You make it now?" Then he got ready to jump.

HOUND DOG:

We're all just standing back here watching. There's nothing we can do, you know. We just hoped and kind of held our breath.

MOE:

I was watching the tires. I mean, it's going to take the tires and go. If he would have come any further, it would have. Finally he stopped and said, "Jump in." I looked. No way. I said, "It's too far. You need to come a little bit more." I didn't want to miss, because goddamn, if I do, I'm going down instantly.

I more or less dove into it. I didn't roll into it, I just went headfirst, with my hands out. I felt that hard steel and slid right into the back of the bucket and stayed there until they got me across where they were.

Moe's return was the first moment of triumph they'd had in many hours. Moe admitted that if Flathead had arrived a minute later, it would have been too late: "My third step into the water would probably have been my last."

BOOGIE:

When we got Moe back, Randy was really relaxed. He knows that we're all together now, we're all going to go as a team. We're all going to drown or we're all going to get out of this mess somehow.

MOE:

I was a happy man, yeah. Man, let me tell you. Of course the other guys were in a different mood. I'm bullshitting with John Unger and I couldn't figure out why he's not saying much. I didn't know the shit they just went through.

It took me a while to figure out what was going on. I had just gotten out of one situation—and now I was trapped again. But at least I was with my buddies.

This map, published in the Pittsburgh *Post-Gazette*, gives a good visual representation of what it looked like inside the Quecreek mine. The graphic is not drawn to scale, however: the passageways in the mine are actually much narrower in comparison with the coal pillars. Also, Dennis Hall's shuttle car, pictured here in a cross-cut between entries five and six, was actually directly behind the miner, heading straight down entry six, at the time of the break-through.

Nine men out

How a crew of Somerset County coal miners became trapped in a flooded shaft, then hung on for 78 hours while the world rooted for their rescue.

Graphic by Daniel Marsula, James Hilston and Ted Crow/Post-Gazette

Workers check a drill bit being used to bore an escape hole,
Friday morning, July 26.

(STEVE HELBER, AP/WIDE WORLD PHOTOS)

A rescue worker listens as he holds a microphone cable and hears the miners' voices, Saturday, July 27.

(STEVE HELBER, AP/WIDE WORLD PHOTOS)

Randy Fogle is helped out of the rescue capsule, Sunday, July 28.

(GUY WATHEN, AP/WIDE WORLD PHOTOS)

Blaine Mayhugh is helped out.

Thomas Foy is rescued.

(GUY WATHEN, AP/WIDE WORLD PHOTOS)

Miners on the surface reach out to shake hands with John Unger as he is lifted from the hole in the capsule.

(AP/WIDE WORLD PHOTOS)

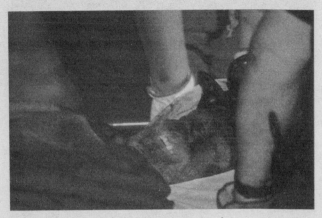

Ronald Hileman is rescued.

(GENE J. PUSKAR, AP/WIDE WORLD PHOTOS)

John Phillippi is rescued.

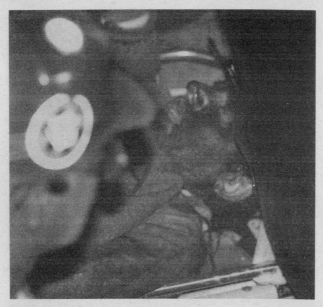

Robert Pugh is carried to the medical tent.

Rescue workers celebrate as Mark Popernack nears the surface.

(STEVE HELBER, AP/WIDE WORLD PHOTOS)

Mark Popernack gives a thumbs-up as he is lifted to the surface.

(STEVE HELBER, AP/WIDE WORLD PHOTOS)

Workers hook equipment to a drill used to create an escape tunnel.

(GENE J. PUSKAR, AP/WIDE WORLD PHOTOS)

Miners (*l to r*) Larry Summerville, Doug Custer, and Jim Weiland embrace after their coworkers were rescued Sunday, July 28.

(GENE J. PUSKAR, AP/WIDE WORLD PHOTOS)

8 · BUILDING WALLS

THE MEN GATHERED at the bolter at the top of entry four. It was, for the moment, high and dry. Several hours had passed since the breakthrough. The machine was still warm, providing a small but welcome comfort to Randy and his crew as they leaned against it. They had no idea what was going on aboveground. Did anyone know they were trapped in there? Had the other crew gotten out, or were they all dead? Was there already a rescue operation in progress, or were the rescuers going to wait until morning to get started?

These thoughts were all the more urgent because the air in the mine was now thick and stifling. The water had cut off the ventilation system. There was no circulation, nothing coming in from outside. Their chests were heaving; they felt weak and light-headed. Several of them walked over to a quiet spot and threw up.

BOOGIE:

Randy said there was only one drill that he knows of that can drill a hole big enough to get us out, and that's in Arkansas. And we're thinking, Jeez, Arkansas, that's a long ways from here. Randy said he thinks in twelve hours they can have it anywhere they want. I'm thinking, We don't got twelve hours. And he said, "Yeah, Arkansas is the only drill I know." Randy kept assuring us, telling us that there's good people that's trying to get us out of here. I wanted to believe him. And I said, "Just think, boys, we'll be on Channel 6 news tonight."

FLATHEAD:

I got on the scoop and we went down entry five, trying to see if we could escape that way. Nothing. We went down the intake and checked the doors. I mean, you would open it just a crack and the water rushed in. We just checked a couple of them and then Randy said, "Let's head back up." And when we got there, he said, "Okay, we're going to start building walls."

Building walls is an old coal miner's survival strategy after a cave-in or roof fall. By barricading themselves in a small area, miners can protect themselves from further collapse and conserve body heat; they can thus bide their time while they await rescuers.

In this case, building walls might help Randy's crew keep the rising water off them for a few extra hours. But barricading oneself in, as every coal miner knows, is also an admission of defeat, and the first step toward a long, slow death by suffocation or drowning. These guys weren't afraid of dying, but they didn't want to do it slowly.

Before they started the walls, they needed a decent supply of drinking water. There was of course water all around, but nobody wanted to drink it. (As it later turned out, they could have—it might have given them indigestion, nothing worse.) Luckily, there were twelve jugs of distilled water for the machinery stockpiled not far away, which they grabbed with the scoop.

BLAINE:

Deep down, you knew the walls weren't going to hold the water back. You have to try, there's always a chance. But you know, if that water wants to come in, it's going to come in.

BOOGIE:

It was tough. I remember taking a deep breath, talking to the guys about building walls, then taking another deep breath, saying a few more words. Every breath was a struggle. You had to use your mouth and really pull it in. I was sure we was going to suffocate.

UNGER:

I said, "Fogle, I don't think they're going to get to us in time, man. I think this is too big." "Oh, they're going to get us," he'd say. "They're going to get us." He would always tell me that.

TUCKER:

I didn't mind the hard breathing. I figured, buddy, if we're going to go, this is the way we do want to go. Because we know this water down here is going to be coming up sooner or later. You're looking at maybe thirty to sixty crosscuts.

BOOGIE:

I wasn't worried about drowning at first. I thought maybe the pumps would pump everything out and the water would quit running. I told the guys, "Them old-timers never went that far in the mines. Don't worry about it, we'll be okay. The water's going to slow down, ain't even going to fill half the mine up." I didn't realize this old mine was six, seven miles deep.

BLAINE:

When we decided to start building walls, Randy sent me to change the scoop batteries so we'd have plenty of power.

I had to go down about twenty-five crosscuts, and when I got down there, my scoop charger was underwater. I had to turn around. When I came back, I told Randy, "We've got twenty-five walls left." At the rate it was coming in, I figured that meant eight or ten hours.

They planned to build four walls between the entries and the crosscuts, each about seventy feet long and the same height as the mine (four and a half feet), making a rectangular enclosure about a hundred feet by a hundred and fifty feet. The walls were dry-laid with concrete cinder block (frequently used in mines, and stockpiled nearby), then coated with thick sealant, which they applied with their hands. This was tough work under the best of circumstances, but under these conditions, it was downright brutal.

BLAINE:

When it came to the wall building, I basically took charge. At one point, Moe even told me, "Blaine, you've got to slow down and save your energy." And I'm, like, "Fuck it, I want to get these walls built. I ain't going out like this."

The first wall took an hour, maybe longer. The bad air, the hard work, and the cold quickly took its toll on the men. The second wall was even slower. While Blaine and the others struggled, Randy, Harpo, Hound Dog, and Tucker retreated up to the bolter to rest. A few of them dozed off.

FLATHEAD:

I had been running around like a nut until then. Now I couldn't breathe; I had a bad headache and was sick in the stomach. I did a little bit of work, but I just couldn't do much because it felt so miserable and my chest hurt. So I just laid in the scoop there and those guys built two walls. Then I got up and helped them get some more blocks.

Before long, Blaine, Boogie, and Unger were the only guys still throwing up blocks.

MOE:

I had to take a break. That lack of oxygen, buddy, it breaks you down. I mean, everybody was kicked in the ass.

Poor Tucker was really having a rough time. He laid up at the bolter by himself for a while. Randy even told me, "I'm worried about Tom—he's in bad shape." And I yelled up at him a couple times: "Tom, you all right?" "Yeah, buddy," he'd call back. He was just laying up there, trying to absorb some heat.

UNGER:

Randy said his heart hurt really, really bad. I said, "You surely aren't going to die on us, are you? I'm going to hate it if you die, because we're going to be in a lot of trouble." And he said, "No, but it really hurts." And Tucker, you know, he had heart trouble, too. [Tucker had recently had two stents put in to open clogged arteries.] Randy asked him if had any nitro with him and Tucker said, "No, it's up above." I thought, Of all the times to forget all his stuff.

I said, "Whatever you do, Fogle, don't die, man. We need you really bad."

Randy and his crew had no way of knowing, but aboveground, the rescue operation was just getting started. One of the first workers to the site was Bob Long, a local surveyor, who was awakened at about 11:30 P.M. by a phone call and rushed to the site. Long is a suntanned thirty-seven-year-old with a bad-boy attitude and a fondness for gold chains. When he arrived, he met immediately with Joe Gallo, the mine engineer at the Quecreek mine and the secretary and treasurer of PBS Coal, and Dave Rebuck, the president of Black Wolf Coal. Their outlook, Long says, was bleak: "[Gallo and Rebuck] were freaked. Everybody was freaked. At that point, I was thinking bodies. Gallo looked at me and he had a shit-scared look on his face. I know he was thinking bodies, too."

Gallo and Rebuck, who were in contact with the Pennsylvania Department of Environmental Protection's deep mine rescue team, knew that the first thing they had to do was get air to the trapped men. The only practical way to do that was to drill a 6-inch hole from the surface down to the mine, a distance of about 240 feet.

But where to drill the hole? They had to get the hole down quick; a miscalculation could waste hours of precious time. They knew the area of the mine the crew had been working in, and guessed that the miners had probably retreated to the highest point in that section. They marked several spots on the mine map and decided to let the surveyors pick the best one.

It was Long's job to translate those spots on the map to spots on the ground. Using a high-tech global positioning system (GPS) similar to the one that the U.S. military uses to guide smart bombs, Long and his boss, Sean Isgan, tracked the coordinates until they led them to the middle of a field just off Route 985, a busy two-lane road into Somerset. They quickly discovered that, of the three potential drill spots, only one in the area was easily accessible by drilling rigs.

BOB LONG:

It was just an open field. Nobody around. We're out there in the dark trying to locate this spot when a guy in a truck pulls up and comes at us with a .45 pistol in his hand. He says, "What the fuck is going on?" I recognized him immediately. It was Billy Arnold, the farmer who owns the land. Helluva nice guy. I say, "Billy, chill. It's Bob." I explain what's going on. He just unloaded his gun, threw the clip out, and said, "Do whatever you have to do. If you need to rip my fence down, whatever. I don't care."

So I got my handheld GPS box out, checked the coordinates again, and walked around until I found the spot. I looked at Sean and Sean looked at me and goes, "Is that it, right there?" I was, like, oh, fuck. My ass was sucked up to my throat. So far, it's the middle of the night, it's dark—what if some of the underground survey marks I was using had been off? Sean asked me six hundred times, "Are you sure this is the spot? Are you sure?" I said, "You've trusted me with this goddamn thing for two years. Why would you stop now? This is the spot right here."

MOE:

We was working, we heard this sound above us. Son of a bitch, they're drilling already! It was a good sound.

RANDY:

I knew from how fast it was coming down that it was not a rescue hole. I knew it was either communications or air. You're not going to drill it that fast if it's a rescue hole. Much as we needed the air, what the guys were really hoping for was a telephone. We wanted to tell our wives and families that we were okay. That was top on our minds.

BOOGIE:

That guy punched that hole quick. It took like an hour, an hour and a half. I thought I heard some drilling—bam, it was there. The drill bounced off about a foot off the bottom of the mine. I was standing right beside it when it broke through. Scared the hell out of me.

When they're trapped, miners are trained to communicate by tapping—a sort of miners' Morse code. This code is written on a sticker that every coal miner has inside his hard hat, although with years of hard use, the stickers often wear away or become illegible.

Randy and the others quickly gathered around the protruding steel bit.

RANDY:

I asked who had a sticker in their hard hat, and Moe had one. I said, "We're gonna get this right." So Moe took off his helmet and we looked inside. You're supposed to hit three times to establish communication, then after they answer, hit once for each guy. And that's what we did—three taps, then when they answered, we hit it nine times again.

MOE:

Tuck banged on with his hammer, then I banged on with mine. From then on, everything was nine—every time we bang on this pipe it's nine times, or any time we banged on the roof is nine times. We wanted to be sure they knew there was nine of us alive down here.

BOOGIE:

I heard them banging in response. "Come here, boys, listen to this," I said. It was clear as a bell—they were answering us.

A few minutes later, with no warning at all, a screaming came out of the hole, causing the guys to jump back. It was fresh air, heated to 190 degrees and blown in under such tremendous pressure that it blew out one of the walls they had just built.

BOOGIE:

Man, that air was loud. We had to stand near it to build the walls, and I could barely do it. It was like a shrieking sound. But yeah, you could breathe a lot better now.

We thought, Hey, if nothing else, we ain't going to suffocate.

9 · SIPESVILLE

THE SIPESVILLE FIREHOUSE is located on a quiet road just a mile or two from where the men were trapped. It's a nice old wooden structure that looks the way a firehouse in a small town is supposed to look, with white clapboard and a big hall off to one side where bingo games and community dances are held.

That night it was host to a vigil. The wives and kids of the trapped miners sat in stunned silence, trying to make sense of what had happened to their loved ones. A number of tables and chairs had been hastily set up in the hall, hot coffee was brewing in the back kitchen, and already food was beginning to arrive—doughnuts, sandwiches, chips, pizza.

During that chaotic first night, it was hard for family members to get any good information about what was going on. They had no TV (there was one in the hall, but no one turned it on until later) and were dependent upon rumors and the bits of news they heard from friends and family, many of whom knew people involved in the rescue operations and would call the fire hall with updates.

In the early hours, family briefings were short and vague. Doug Custer, who had escaped earlier from the mine, tried to keep the families informed, but he was quickly overwhelmed by the job. Dave Rebuck, owner of Black Wolf Coal, stopped in to talk with the families, but didn't offer much new information. Rescuers were understandably more focused on figuring out how to get the men out than they were on keeping the families fully informed.

By dawn Thursday, the only real hard facts that most family members knew was that the men had somehow cut into the old Saxman mine, and that between fifty and sixty million gallons of water (it was later determined to be closer to seventy million gallons) had flooded into the mine where they were working. The essential question, of course, was: Were the men alive?

Had these families been able to turn on a TV at about 7 A.M., they would have heard CNN broadcasting the news that rescuers had picked up the tapping sounds underground. And had the families known that, it might have brought some relief and hope. But they did not know that—at least, for a while.

MISSY PHILLIPPI:

I was mad as hell that we weren't being told anything. We heard about the sixty million gallons of water that flooded the mine, and that was about it. At seven that morning, I called a friend of ours that works in the mine because I just knew they weren't going to tell us the truth about what had happened. And then I took Doug [Custer] outside. It was just me and him. I said, "I want you to tell me straight. I don't want you to beat around the bushes. Nobody is here but me and you." I said, "Please, Doug." He got tears in his eyes. He said, "It's not good, Missy."

SUE UNGER:

I spent most of that first night with Ron Hileman's wife, Cathy. She was the only person I really knew there. At first I was pretty hopeful. I'm thinking, They're going to get him out, and I'll just throw him in the car and we'll come home. It didn't work out that way, especially when they started talking about water. I wasn't concerned because they didn't say it was a cave-in or anything, and I thought if it's water, they had a better chance. I don't know. I don't know anything about a mine. I just had this feeling that they were coming out. Some of the wives wanted the guys who were briefing us to tell us more, to keep us better informed, but there was really nothing to tell us.

MISSY PHILLIPPI:

They made you feel stupid, like when they would say things to you, like—what the hell is the word? *Inundated.* Well, it's flooded to me. You know, when they would say stuff, you didn't know what they were saying. And nobody would ask a question because some of them didn't know what the hell they were talking about.

So we really had no understanding of what the hell was going on. For a woman, I think, even if your husband works in a mine for thirty years, if you've never been in there and never worked it, how do you know all that? I felt that way, too, like they were thinking, They're just dumb wives, we can just tell them anything and they'll believe it.

I felt like I had a real responsibility there, a real job to do. John and I had talked about him getting trapped in a mine because, you know, over the years, things had happened. And I always told him, "Honey, I'd never leave you down there, I'd make them get you out. I wouldn't leave you." That's what I always told him. Because I'm claustrophobic as hell. "I'll make them get you out," I always told him. "I'll dig."

SUE UNGER:

It was kind of hard to fill in the time because, you know, waiting and waiting is really a hard thing. But as soon as someone would walk in, the room would get real quiet, and everyone kind of sat on the edge of their seats, waiting to hear what was happening.

I spent most of the night with Cathy [Hileman]. Her daughters were there, too. And we just kind of talked about different things. We didn't really even talk about what was going on or anything. We just kind of tried to talk about other stuff. And then about six in the morning, I thought, Well, maybe I better call somebody. So I called my sister and told her to tell my parents and call the minister and put him on the prayer chain.

That first night, while I was sitting there with the Hileman family, Mike Dunlap—he's a local preacher, I don't even know what church he's affiliated with—was talking with some of the families. One of the ladies said, "We should get Mike to lead us in prayer."

So she went over and asked him. And he says, "In times like this, a lot of us like to have prayer. If you're not comfortable with this, maybe you'd like to step out." Because he didn't know what kind of people were there, so he handled it very well. And then he had a prayer over us. And then after that, we just continued to have prayer periodically, with different ministers or priests leading us.

John Weir, a land manager for PBS Coal, usually spends his time trying to secure coal rights for PBS. He's a big, rough-edged guy, six foot four, with a graying mustache and glasses. Like many of the guys who work for the mines, he's a big hunter and gun lover. He keeps a small-caliber pistol in his pocket, and a .357 Magnum stashed in his silver Dodge Dakota pickup.

Weir had spent most of Wednesday night securing old maps of the Saxman mine to help rescuers understand what they were dealing with. In the early morning, Dave Rebuck approached him. "'We need someone to go over to the fire hall and keep the families updated,'" Weir recalls. "'You want to take care of that?' I volunteered for the job, having no idea what I was getting into."

Like everyone else, Weir was caught up in the emotion of the rescue. He knew many of the men down there and had suffered through a horrific mining accident himself, when he had been nearly killed when another worker accidentally clubbed him in the head with a sledgehammer. In those early hours, Weir did his best to lay out the general situation at the rescue site, telling the families that the air hole was now finished, the men were getting air, and a larger drill rig was headed to the site from West Virginia to begin drilling the rescue hole.

But as to the question of whether the men were alive or dead, Weir added little. "He said he didn't know," recalls Missy Phillippi. Which, as Weir later agreed, was not exactly true: He had in fact been at the site when the rescue workers heard the miners tapping early that morning. "I was standing right there and heard it loud and clear," he says. But when he first arrived at the firehouse, he didn't tell the families this. "I don't know why," he admits. "I just didn't. Maybe I didn't want to get their hopes up. Looking back, it was probably a mistake."

JOHN WEIR:

The first time I walked in the firehouse, I didn't expect that many people there. There were, I don't know, sixty, seventy. I also didn't expect to see the sadness. I didn't expect the questions, the confrontations—they wanted to be told everything. I mean, there was some screaming goin' on in there.

MISSY PHILLIPPI:

On Thursday morning sometime, John Weir came in, and he was hemming and hawing again. And he's not a public speaker, for one. He was almost in tears. He was so upset and everything.

I looked at him and thought, Don't be sugarcoating it and stuff, and don't be pussyfooting around. He was ready to bust out crying. I know what he's thinking. He thought they were dead, too. It's all he could do to stand there and face us all.

And that's when I stood up and said, "I don't speak

for everybody here, but I think I speak for the majority." I said, "Don't be pussyfooting around and spitting and sputtering. Just say what you need to say, get it out." And I just sorta went on and on. I was angry. I was mad. I didn't understand why they were treating us like this, keeping information from us, not telling everything they knowed. These were our husbands down there; we had a right to know what was going on.

At that point, I had no idea if they were doing everything they could or not. Because they hadn't offered to take us up there or nothing. They would come in and they would say stuff, but a lot of it made no sense to me, because they didn't show you a picture or draw any diagrams or do anything to make it easier to understand. All I could think of was fifty million gallons of water, and it's four feet high in the mine.

So I told all this to John. And then whenever I got hot under the collar, I jumped up and started waving my arms. I wasn't going to attack him. He's, like, six-five, you know, I'm only four-eleven.

John was spitting and sputtering so bad, he was ready to burst out crying. I don't even know what he said. And he's, like, "Well, we're, you know, trying our best." And I'm like—I just wanted to go nuts. I didn't trust him, I didn't trust the company. And I thought my husband was dead.

[96]

Distrust between owners and workers runs deep in the coal industry. You can trace it all the way back to the crusades of Mother Jones and the West Virginia labor riots in the 1920s. Missy's own bitterness and distrust had been building for years. "PBS Coal used to treat their workers really well, like family," she says. "Wives would get together for dinners, we all knew each other. But then a few years ago, everything changed. They started making John [Flathead] work ten-hour days, six days a week, while at the same time cutting benefits and never giving any kind of pay raise." What really got to Missy was a card the company sent out at Christmas one year. "On the front, they announced they were giving everyone a thirty-five-cent-an-hour raise. Then you turned to the next page, and they tell us we have to start paying for our own benefits—ten percent of medical, I think it was. I couldn't believe it. Do they think we are stupid or what?"

MISSY PHILLIPPI:

After my outburst, I left because I felt I embarrassed myself. And I went clear up to the corner of the parking lot behind the fire hall. My sister-in-law was with me. And I started to cry. I just said, "I don't want to be a widow at thirty-four and raise a twelve-year-old son by myself. What am I going to do?"

Randy Fogle's mother came up. She's an old lady, a

tough old lady. She's sweet, though. She says, "Honey, you did really good. I'm glad." She was rubbing my head, and I started crying.

SANDY POPERNACK:

When Missy started in, I'm thinking, I'm embarrassed. I can't believe this lady is doing this. I left, I walked out. I thought, You know, they're doing what they can do. Give them a break. I mean, I was still on my first twenty-four hours and I was still thinking they're okay. Of course, then after it got a little longer, then I got a little miffed and started wondering about how much they were telling us.

ANNETTE FOGLE:

Missy just wanted straight answers, and she felt that we weren't getting straight answers. Actually, I think we all felt like that. Well, I won't speak for the other wives, but I know there was times that I felt that they were telling us one thing and then you was hearing something else from somebody else. And then they would come back in and say what that other person had said. So you felt that they weren't telling you everything that was going on.

JOHN WEIR:

When I came out of the fire hall after all this, the first thing I did, I called my wife. I said, "Holy shit, what did I get myself into here?" And she said, "Hey, do what you can, and call me whenever you need to. And remember what happened when your dad was killed." My dad got killed in the steel mills. And no one was telling us anything while he was laying in the hospital, but he only made it twelve hours. Every doctor that walked by, you thought they should stop and tell you something. And there was nothing to tell. So I tried to just focus on that, and it kinda got me through.

It was not until Thursday afternoon, almost eight hours after Randy and his crew had first pounded nine times on the air pipe, that families were finally able to figure out what was going on.

ANNETTE FOGLE:

That afternoon sometime, Mike Wolf, my son's girl-friend's dad, had been home. And he came into the fire-house and said, "Annette, it's on CNN, there was nine taps." And I said, "But they're telling us that there was no taps." He said, "I'm telling you, it was on CNN there had been nine taps on that pipe."

Mike said he couldn't understand it, because he said John Weir was the one that was talking on CNN. And I couldn't understand it neither.

LESLIE MAYHUGH:

I had gone home because the kids needed warmer clothes for in the mornings because they were cold. And I knew while they were there, they needed shorts, because during the day it was hot. And I'm up there with a worn-out white T-shirt, a pullover Jets sweatshirt, and a pair of sweatpants. So I'm not feeling real comfortable running around.

When I got home, I walked around the empty house for a few minutes, looking in all the rooms. I figured if Blaine was dead, he'd give me some kind of sign. I'd feel a breeze or something, something unusual, something that told me he was trying to communicate with me and tell me that he was gone. But I didn't feel nothing like that. The house felt just the same.

Then I get a call from some friends. They're like, "They heard tapping." I said, "What are you talking about?" And they're, like, "Leslie, they heard tapping." I said, "You're kidding me?" They say no, they think they heard nine taps. But another friend said five taps, which is in their hats, their helmets, some distress code. And of course I thought five—that means five guys. And I'm, like, with my luck, two of mine would be in the four that didn't make it. And then I heard later that there was nine taps, definitely nine.

And so I called my mom and I said, "Guess what, they heard tapping. Put on your news. CNN is coming across live."

And that lifted us up for a while. We felt like, "Yes, this is good!"

10 · SWAMPED

Now that they could breathe, Randy and his crew had the luxury of considering what was going to happen to them next. The sweet relief of the air was undercut by lingering disappointment that the rescue crew still had not dropped down a phone, a radio, anything. Not knowing what was going on and not being able to tell their families that they were still alive seemed a form of torture. "A lot of the guys kept complaining about that," Randy says. "'Why no phone? Why no communication?' And I just told them, 'They can't.' I explained the whole deal to them, what they were trying to do."

The truth is, Randy himself wasn't exactly sure what was going on. But he was smart enough not to let his crew know that: "Keeping morale up, that was the most important thing," he says. He surmised that the rescuers were trying to create a kind of pressurized air bubble underground that would keep the water back from them. Otherwise, Randy thought, why not drill another hole and drop a phone down?

"That was the only reason I could think of—because they didn't want to break the seal," he says. "So that's what I tried to explain to the guys. They were blowing us an air bubble."

Randy's theory was more or less correct. Rescuers aboveground knew that the greatest danger to the men who were trapped underground was water, not air. John Urosek, a mine ventilation expert who worked for the U.S. Department of Labor's Mine Safety Health Administration, believed that if they pumped a large volume of highly pressurized air into the mine, they might be able to create a pocket of air that would keep the water off the men while they drilled a larger rescue shaft. Urosek's decision was controversial, but with so much water flooding in and so little time, there weren't many alternatives.

Underground, the pressurized air may have slowed the water's advance, but it didn't stop it.

BLAINE:

Some of us were working our asses off to get those walls built. The pressure from the air had blown one of them out, and then we had to start all over on a couple of the walls because of where the air hole came down. We needed to have the air hole inside the walls, so we had to rebuild a couple of them in different spots. It was a ton of work, especially because we were so wet and cold and tired.

The hardest thing was seeing that water coming up. I mean, we could breathe better now, but that water never stopped. We would walk down through the entry and see it and measure it, you know, and it was coming up a couple of crosscuts every hour. Just this slow climb up the mine toward us. So within a couple of hours, we went from thinking we were going to suffocate to thinking we were going to drown.

RANDY:

I kept telling them, "Hey, he's trying to get enough pressure in here to keep the water off of us." But not everyone thought it would work. It was a battle, you know, just to keep morale up. That was a big deal. We were all tired and wet and freezing. Like Unger, I know, figured we was going to die. "John," I says, "I ain't dying in here. I'm getting out." And I never let it get in my head that we weren't going to make it.

MOE:

I remember telling Blaine a couple times, "Just don't worry about it, we'll get out of it. We ain't fucked yet." I didn't know Blaine real well—I just met him when he started in the mine about six or seven months earlier— but I felt me and Blaine was close. We got along good, bullshitted a lot. You know, me and him both fished a lot, and we talked about that. I think he was more worried than anybody. Even when we was working, building walls and stuff, he never stopped. Honestly, he busted his ass. I don't know how he did it. Everybody else was beat from the lack of oxygen, but Blaine never stopped.

BLAINE:

We had too many guys laying around. I wasn't pissed, 'cause I knew a lot of them was older, and their energy was gone then. But still, I wanted to get those walls built, I thought it might save us. I even yelled at the guys resting at the bolter [a long, low drilling rig on rubber wheels, with two braces lifted toward the roof of the mine]. I said, "I don't want to be a fucking dick or whatever, but we've got to get these walls built."

FLATHEAD:

At one point we started running out of bricks for the walls. Me, Hound Dog, and Harpo had knocked the return wall down and we was carrying some of the bricks up by hand. We got that one done, and then we had one more to go. When I went down to grab some more bricks, I saw that the water was way up. I mean, it is gaining, gaining. It was already ankle-deep. Ten, fifteen minutes later, when I went down again, it was up to my waist.

BOOGIE:

I was one of the last of the guys to give in and say we weren't going to make it. I mean, I heard Blaine talk, Hound Dog talk about we ain't going to make it. And I never gave in. I never really gave up hope until we were working on that last wall.

And I think it started out with Blaine laying the block, I think, starting the wall. The water was only about two inches deep at the time. So we laid four or five down flat to start the corner up so we could go across. And Unger came down to me at that time. A lot of the guys were up at the bolter—Hound Dog, Harpo. I don't know where Randy was at. It was just Flathead, me, and Unger came down then and Blaine, starting this wall. And Blaine laid a couple blocks down. I was going to get a couple blocks to lay down. And water was coming in so fast now I couldn't even get my block laid down in the water—they were starting to float. I thought, Jeez, we got to get this wall up. This water was coming up, coming around the corner to us. And the air pipe, you know, was right there, and the noise was so loud, it was just screaming, and I could hardly stand to be near it.

UNGER:

While we was building that last wall, Fogle came down. I said to him, "We've got some big trouble." He looked at the water and he said, "What the hell you been doing?" I said, "What do you mean, what the hell I've been doing?" He was kind of—you know, stressed. I said, "What do you *think* I've been doing? I'm trying to build this wall. And it ain't working."

Boogie looked at me and said, "What are you going to do?" I said, "I don't know. I think I'm going to die, to be honest with you."

We stood there a few minutes. The water's just pouring in. And Randy was trying to throw block up. It was hopeless.

Blaine just looked at us and said, "I'm too young to die." Then he headed up to the bolter.

RANDY:

Blaine asked me if I had a pen. He didn't tell me what it was for, but I knew—he was going to write a note to his family. I didn't say nothing, I just gave him the pen.

BLAINE:

I just quit. I used the excuse I was tired because there was, like, five guys up there at the bolter sleeping and I went up and woke them up and told them, "The water's coming in on the last wall. We're in trouble." But basically, I quit because I wanted the peaceful time. I knew what was coming.

UNGER:

After Boogie and Randy went up to the bolter, I was the last guy down there. I stayed for a while, watching the water pour in. Then I walked up and stopped at the feeder, where there was some dry coal. I sat down in the coal bin for a bit. I was tired and I prayed. I needed to get myself right with God.

II · HOW TO DROWN
WITH DIGNITY

UNGER:

When I walked up to the bolter, the other guys were all there—some sitting, some on their knees. They were all good men, and friends. They've seen you at your best and they've seen you at your worst. And we were at our worst right there. I mean, you were never going to see these guys again, you were never going to work with these guys again. You're never going to talk all kinds of crap that you talk to them or what you ever say to them. Just like poor Harpo, man. As a joke, I used to send rocks home in his bucket all the time. Stupid stuff. I'm not going to be able to do this kind of stuff to these guys anymore. You're looking at everybody and you think, Well, we're all going to die together. This is it. This is the bottom line.

BOOGIE:

I seen death on John Unger's face and Hound Dog's face and Tucker's face. I guess I had it on my face, too—death. We knew at that point we were going to die. Blaine was crying, a lot of us were crying.

Their final refuge was a small area at the top of entry four, thirty feet wide by seventy feet long, with most of that space taken up by the big, heavy bolter. The only light they had were the lamps on their helmets, which they kept off most of the time, and a small lantern—miners call it a bug lamp—that Randy had found. It cast a shadowy light, just enough to illuminate the whites of their eyes and to give a shine to the black coal that pressed in around them.

HOUND DOG:

It was like a bad dream. I was trying to wake up, home in bed with my wife, and say, "Wow, boy, that was some dream." I just could not believe that this was happening. I thought of my brother-in-law, who passed away at age forty-nine. I know how hard that was on the family. And then I'd be another one, forty-nine.

BLAINE:

I thought about fishing with my dad and with my kids. Trips to the lake, the wind blowing, the water rocking the boat.

And I thought about my wife. I told the guys, "I didn't kiss her good-bye today. She was mowing the lawn, and I was late, and I just waved." I always kiss her good-bye, but for some reason, I don't know why, I didn't kiss her that day.

That bothered me a lot. Of all the days not to kiss her, you know?

Blaine ripped up an old resin box (resin is used to secure the roof bolts) that was resting on the bolter and used the cardboard for paper. He switched on his helmet lamp, his hands shaking, and used Randy's pen to compose his final thoughts to his family.

BLAINE:

I'd seen lots of reports of old mine accidents. And they'd say how they found a father and son hugging each other when they dug them up, you know, and they'd have written their farewell letters. And I just remembered that and thought it was a good idea.

I didn't say anything to anyone about what I wrote. And I still haven't.

When I finished, I looked at my watch—it was 11:45 A.M. on Thursday. I wrote the time down on the note. And then after I finished, I asked if anyone else wanted to write something, and everyone's, like, yeah.

So I passed the pen off to my father-in-law, and that's how it started.

TUCKER:

When I started writing the note, I just broke down. I couldn't take it no more.

MOE:

I'm just sitting there thinking, staring at the ground. I didn't want to write that note because I wasn't giving up hope.

But that water kept coming. I took the pen. I was thinking about my family. I was thinking about my kids a lot. I wasn't angry. I was just thinking, Christ, I'm going to die.

My note was short. I made it short because I wanted everybody to have time to write their note and the water was coming really fast.

For Moe, there was some terrible déjà vu in this moment: For the second time in twelve hours, he believed his life was over.

MOE:

This time it was different. This time it was going to happen. When I was on the other side of that water, I had that little bit of hope. Maybe the other guys would come back, maybe I'd figure out a way across the water. But this here was obvious. Our backs were up against the wall. The water was coming up. We were going to drown.

RANDY:

The one thing I thought about when I was writing was that I would never be able to walk my daughter down the aisle. Just the idea of never seeing my family again, that was the worst for me there.

I wish I could have told my kids I loved them more often. I thought of that. And my parents, I wish I could have told them more, which I didn't.

UNGER:

When you write that note, I mean, that's the bottom line. That's as bad as it gets. You've played all your cards. There's no way out.

That was the lowest point for me. I always made a promise to my wife that I would never do that, I would always come out of the mine one way or the other, and that I would never, ever write that letter. But I wrote it.

FLATHEAD:

Blaine grabbed a plastic bucket of bits off the bolter and dumped a whole bucket out on the ground. When we were done, we put all the notes into the bucket and sealed it up with electrical tape. Then we wired it to the bolter so it wouldn't float away.

In making their final preparations for their deaths, there was only one question left: What would happen to their bodies? Almost as nightmarish as the idea of drowning was the idea of their bodies being left to float aimlessly through the caverns and corridors of the mine.

It was Tucker, the mechanical wizard on the crew, the man who could fix anything, who came up with a solution.

TUCKER:

I found a piece of cable from the miner, I don't know, forty feet long or something, and said, "We might as well be all tied together so they don't have to go hunting for our bodies all over the mine and in the mud.

That way they can find us all and we'll be together. It will be easy."

So Tucker tied one end of the cable securely to the bolter (at twenty tons or so, that machine wasn't going anywhere). Then he slipped the cable through his miner's belt and passed it on. Blaine, Hound Dog, Flathead, and Boogie all tied in. Moe, Harpo, Unger, and Randy refused.

MOE:

Somebody said, "Come on, tie up, tie up." And I said, "No, when the water gets up to my waist, I'll tie." I wasn't giving up yet.

UNGER:

I only tied off for a little while, and that was a little bit later. I couldn't handle it. I thought, I'm not doing this.

Their preparations complete, there was nothing to do but wait. At this point, the water was about thirty feet below them. It looked as gentle as a lake, just a big pool of flat black water inching slowly toward them.

Every one of these guys was closely acquainted with death. They had seen friends crushed by roof falls and dismembered by machinery. They had had close calls themselves. Readying yourself for this fate—calculating the odds, playing the angles—was part of what it meant to be a coal miner. It was, in some awful way, the natural course of things.

But nobody had thought about water. Nobody was prepared to drown.

And the terrible irony was, Randy and his crew were all passionate fishermen. Many of the best moments of their lives had been spent out on the water in the lakes around Somerset, hooking bass and bluegill with their sons or fathers.

FLATHEAD:

I wished we'd just run out of air and pass out because I didn't know how I would do this. Are you going to put your head tight to the roof and try to keep as much air in your lungs as you can? Or are you just going to go under?

HOUND DOG:

Boogie and I were probably the closest of all nine people. I went to school with Boog. We graduated together, worked in all different kinds of mines. I've known Boog probably for forty years.

So while we were sitting there, I said to Boog, "Can you believe this? You know, this is it. This is a hell of a way to go." I always thought the mines might take me someday. But I thought it would be a piece of rock there somewhere with my name on it that would come down and smash me. I always kind of thought that, but never drowning. I don't know about you, but I think that would be one hell of a way to go.

HARPO:

I had my own ideas about this. I wasn't going to sit there and wait for that water to come up on me and drown me. That's why I wouldn't tie myself with everybody, because I wasn't going to sit there and listen to all of my buddies, my family, choke and gag. I wasn't going to listen to that. I was going to take my last breath and dive in, and when my body figured it needed more air to come up, I ain't going to get none, I'm gone.

BOOGIE:

All I kept thinking about is getting myself up against the wall of coal and breathing my last breath of air. That was on my mind a lot. I told the guys, I don't want to drown. I hate water to start with. I like to swim and I love to fish, but I hate water. That's the worst thing there is, drowning.

So I kept thinking about how I was going to do

this. Because I'm a Catholic. Harpo said, "Boys, when it comes up to our necks, don't mind me, I'm just going to slip under." And I thought maybe that was suicide by slipping under. And Catholics don't believe in suicide. So I figured, I'm going to raise my head and breathe the last air I can breathe and maybe a miracle will happen. But I ain't going under until I have to.

MOE:

How do you drown with dignity? We talked about it. People fall out of boats and they drown, but when you know it's going to happen to you, how do you make yourself drown? Am I going to just start swallowing this water? Because nobody ever takes water into their lungs on purpose. So how do you do that? Do you inhale it like a cigarette? That's what I was thinking. Do I inhale this water like a cigarette? I decided that when it got up to my neck, I was going to swim out. I never said nothing. But that's what I decided. Who wants to struggle for that last breath? You're going to die. There's no hope. You ain't going to survive in that much water, even if it would quit coming up, for very long.

BOOGIE:

At that moment, boy, a lot of stuff ran through my mind. Like my last spring gobbler I ever killed—it had a ten-inch beard. I was proud of that. I'm fifty years old. My kids graduated. I'm trying to make myself feel better before I die, you know. I'm thinking about the funeral, about what day they're going to find us.

FLATHEAD:

I was thinking, Hell, I'm going to die here and never going to see my wife and son again. This is his first year of hunting. I'm never going to get to go hunting with him and—he's my boy, you know. My boy. At that time I wasn't a firm believer in God, and I'm thinking, Man, I'm going to go to hell and the rest of my family is going to be in heaven.

So then I started praying.

For most of the guys, their final reckoning was a private one. But just as Blaine had taken the lead in writing a note to his family, he also took the lead in opening up about his deepest fears.

UNGER:

We were sitting there and Blaine said, "Hey, John." I said, "What?" "I've got a question to ask you, and you're the only one that can answer this for me."

"Okay," I said. "How heavy is this?" He said, "Well, I want to ask you this and you decide." So I said,

"Okay." He said, "I'm not baptized, John. Do you think I'll go to heaven?"

It was heavy, you know. He was crying. What are you going to say? "Well, nope, some big news for you, Blaine. You're going to hell, buddy. You're history, you're going to burn. You're toast." Plus, you don't want him flipping out down there. You don't want everybody going over the edge.

So I thought about it and I was sincere when I answered him. I said, "Well, Blaine, this is only in my world. But in John Unger's world, I truly and honestly believe that God loves you whether you're baptized or not. You're a good guy, you try to do what's right. And I really truly believe that God will take care of us, and that you will go to heaven. From the bottom of my heart, I believe that."

BLAINE:

Unger made me feel a little better. The one thing I asked God—I wanted to get a glimpse of my family before I was gone. I hoped it would be like the movies, you know, when your soul rises up through the air and you can see what's down below. I just wanted one quick look, I just wanted to know that my family was okay.

As the water rose—it was now about twenty feet away—Randy and his crew were confronted by a final dilemma.

Were they going to stay there at the bolter and let the water rise over them, or would they scramble to the highest ground in the mine—a small area a few hundred feet away, in the back of entry one? It was only a few feet higher, but it would buy them a few more breaths of air. As Moe puts it, "If water comes up on a mouse, he's going to keep running until he's out of water. So will any animal. To me, it was instinct."

MOE:

I finally said, "Randy, we got to go to one." He's, like, "Yeah, we got to go to one." And he told everybody to get up, they were moving to higher ground over in entry one. I think somebody said, "What the hell for? We're going to die anyway." And Randy said, "No, we're going to one, it ain't over yet." He always encouraged us. Randy don't give up.

FLATHEAD:

I was thinking, We're just going to go over there and sit for another five, ten, fifteen minutes and prolong the agony. What's the difference? I mean, we can die here, or we'll go over there and wait to die.

HARPO:

I was having a hard time with this. You know you're going to die, it's just a matter of time. "You know what, guys," I said, "I read the paper every day, but I probably read it different than you guys. I look at the front page and then I flip it over and I look at the obituaries. The only difference, the paper tomorrow is going to have our names in it."

MOE:

My opinion, just my opinion, is that some of the guys just gave up then. They were tired, cold, and they'd had enough. They was going to drown right there and they wasn't going to go to higher ground. I didn't understand that.

Randy and Moe got their way. One of the guys unwired the bucket of notes from the bolter; then they all headed over to entry one. The guys who were cabled together remained tied, duck-walking through the mine like a hunchbacked chain gang.

MOE:

When we left the bolter, the mood changed a little. I don't know why. But as we were walking, Blaine cracked a joke that made everybody laugh. He just looked at us and said, "Any of you guys want to have sex before we die?"

12 · DRILLING AND PUMPING

RESCUE OFFICIALS cautioned family members that news of the nine taps didn't necessarily mean that all nine men were alive. Maybe they misinterpreted the taps—it could have been three taps, three times. It could have been some other signal or simply random pounding. And they warned the families that the situation underground was still dire. The water was still flooding into the mine and showed no signs of letting up.

It didn't matter. There was no denying the hope and optimism that briefly filled the fire hall that Thursday afternoon. "At least we knew they weren't all dead," Leslie recalls. "At least we knew that someone was alive down there, and they still had a chance to get out of the mine alive."

Pennsylvania governor Mark Schweiker had arrived at the rescue site around noon, and after being briefed by rescue workers at the site, made his way over to the fire hall. Governor Schweiker, who had become governor after Tom Ridge resigned ten months earlier to join the Bush administration as director of homeland security, was a virtual unknown to most of the families before this. But his affable style, his can-do optimism, and his penchant for blue denim shirts would win him many admirers in the coming hours—as well as a few detractors.

Governor Schweiker, with help from rescue workers and officials from the state's Department of Environmental Protection, briefed the families on the next phase of the rescue operations. They had considered every possible option, including sending scuba divers into the mine. But they ruled that out after realizing that the divers would have to swim a mile and a half into the mine in cold black water, full of all kinds of hazards, corridors, and unpredictable currents. Then what would they do with the miners once they reached them?

A rescue hole was the only way. Governor Schweiker explained that a superdrill—the word sounded like it was coined by someone on the governor's PR team—had just arrived at the site from Shinnston, West Virginia. The drill could cut a 29-inch hole in solid rock and was at that very moment being set up. It was a slow process: The drilling rig and its support equipment arrive on five different trucks and require a complex network of air compressors and water lines to be set up before the rig begins operation. In addition, a steel sleeve had to be installed in the top twenty feet of the hole, then set in concrete, to help circulate air around the drill bit. Because of all this, the actual drilling was not expected to begin until about 7:30 P.M.

Once the hole was drilled, a 22-inch-wide rescue capsule would be lowered into the mine and would bring the men up one by one. The capsule had been designed in the 1970s for just such a tricky mine rescue, but no one at the site had any experience using it or any idea how well it would work.

This rescue plan was presented to the families as if it were a fairly straightforward operation. In fact, it was enormously difficult and risky. These big rigs, normally used to probe for natural gas, work more like hammers than conventional drills. Using a rapid piston-like motion, they crush the rock, rather than auger through it. Different types of rock require different drilling techniques (limestone is common in this region, and brutally difficult to hammer through), and if you try to push it too hard too fast, the bit could get jammed or break. The hole had to be plumb-straight, too; if it wasn't, it'd be almost impossible to lower the rescue capsule down into the mine. Normally, a big hole like this takes three or four days to drill. Governor Schweiker told the families they'd have it done in about eighteen hours.

Just as important as the drilling, however, was getting

the water pumped out of the mine. At the moment, the only thing keeping Randy and his crew from being swamped was the warm air being blown into the mine at more than 350 pounds per square inch of pressure, creating an air bubble in the highest corner of the mine. If they tried to open a rescue hole before the water level went down, they risked popping the bubble and instantly drowning the men.

So it was imperative to get the water under control. Governor Schweiker told the families that an eighteen-wheeler was rushing five big pumps down from Bridgeport, Connecticut, under a police escort. Powered by 425-horse-power engines, these huge pumps were capable of pumping 5,000 gallons of water per minute, and were usually used to empty shipping canals. A number of smaller pumps had already been set up at the mine entrance, where the water was quickly creating a ten-foot-deep-and-rising lake in what had once been an open pit, submerging machinery and most of the mine maintenance building. In addition, several dewatering holes were also being drilled into the lower por-tions of the mine so that submersible pumps could be dropped down. Once all the pumps were up and running, the rescue team hoped to be able to empty the water out of the mine faster than it was pouring in, thus beginning to lower the water level.

For the families, joy soon faded to apprehension. Before they heard the taps, some had feared that this was already a recovery mission. The hell was simply in waiting to find out if their loved ones were dead or alive. Now that it was clearly a rescue operation, every hour was precious. As Blaine's father, Blaine Mayhugh, Sr., put it, "This was now a race against time."

Thursday afternoon, the families got their first chance to visit the rescue site. When they arrived, they saw a cow pasture that had been transformed into a frantic tableau of big men and big machinery. The rescue hole itself was just a few hundred feet behind an old farmhouse. There were two huge equipment barns on the slope above, and a tall blue silo with an American flag painted on the top. Cows poked their noses through the electric fence nearby, and a black mutt wandered around, sweetly oblivious to what was at stake, looking for someone to scratch its ears.

Overhead, news choppers hovered, kicking up dust when they banked in for a close-up. A half dozen heavy air compressors roared. The big rig that would drill the first rescue hole, which was known to Duane Yost, the contractor who was doing the drilling, simply as rig 18, was already standing tall, nearly ready to begin cutting into the earth.

ANNETTE FOGLE:

When they first asked if we wanted to visit the site, I didn't want to go. My son Matthew talked me into it.

He kept saying, "Mom, I really think you need to go over there."

So we took a small bus from the fire hall. Maybe twenty of us were in it. When we got there, they tried to explain what was going on. If we had any questions, we could ask them. But there was so much noise there that you couldn't hear what they were trying to explain to you. I mean, it was loud.

While I was out there, all that went through my mind was the fact that there's 240 feet of dirt there, and underneath it all is Randy. That's what I thought. I mean, I didn't need to understand those drills and all of that. I knew they were getting the air down, I knew that the big drill was there, too. I didn't need to understand how it worked. I just wanted them to get the hole down and get them out of there. So going out to the site was not much help. I felt worse because I kept staring at that dirt and kept thinking, He's down there.

LESLIE MAYHUGH:

I didn't want to go out to the site, but something told me I had to. When I got there, I just sat on the back of an ambulance and watched. I could see down into the area where they were getting the rig set up, and all the equipment they were bringing in. And that's when I thought, What am I doing here? I wanted to go down and touch the ground above where the guys were trapped, but they wouldn't let me near it.

SANDY POPERNACK:

That fire hall was the most depressing place I'd ever seen in my life. I really needed to get out of there for a while. When I was in there, I had a very pessimistic view of what was happening. I just thought, There's no way that he can be alive. Then I went to that site and saw everyone working so hard. Everyone seemed so positive that he was coming out of there alive. I felt a lot better.

For some of the younger children, the trip to the rescue site was their first chance to see for themselves what had happened to their fathers.

SANDY POPERNACK:

My sons, Daniel and Lucas, both wanted to see the site. Lucas is ten, Daniel is nine. They're both close with their dad, but Lucas particularly. You know how most kids write about their mom when they have to do something in school? Lucas wrote about his dad every time. Like for Valentine's Day, he was his dad's valentine. I always got kind of offended, thinking, What's wrong with this picture? But everything was his dad. He just adores him.

So I took them both down there. I pointed to the air pipe that was going down and said, "That's what's giving Daddy air, so that Daddy can breathe." I pointed to the big rig, the drill, and just explained to them exactly what it was and how it worked, and tried to keep it as simple as I could. My niece was with us, and she was helping to explain, too.

Then after we had been out there a while, I said, "Okay, I'm going to take you guys back to the fire hall." Right then and there, Daniel lost it. I mean, he just started crying. Lucas did fine—he held very strong for me.

Most of the families returned to the fire hall and stayed there, but both Sandy and Missy ended up going back to the site after they dropped their kids off with relatives. Rescue officials had asked all family members to remain in the fire hall, but in a situation like this, neither Sandy nor Missy was too interested in taking orders from anyone. Sandy would end up returning to the fire hall later that night, but Missy was at the site for the long haul: "I wasn't going to leave until they brought my husband up, dead or alive."

MISSY PHILLIPPI:

On Thursday night, I watched one driller work for about seven hours. I mean, he was moving. He was hip-hopping. He was up and down and every which way. I've never seen a man work so hard. He made me tired just lookin' at him. So I laid down on the bank, and I could hear that drill, and I could feel my mind drifting. I was thinking about my son and what was going to happen to us. Then I fell asleep.

After the drilling began at about 7:30 P.M., there was nothing for the families to do but wait. John Weir held an impromptu briefing every hour or so in the fire hall, keeping them up to date on the foot-by-foot progress of the drilling and pumping. Food kept arriving from local restaurants—pizza from Pizza Hut, lasagna from the Oakhurst Tea Room, boxes of eclairs and old-fashioneds from Dunkin' Donuts, sandwiches from Eat 'N Park. Fried chicken, sandwiches, cases of soda, coffee, juice, Power Bars, cakes, pies—you name it, they had it. Nobody was going hungry during this ordeal.

Thursday turned out to be a hot, humid night, and it was even hotter in the fire hall. After Weir's briefings, a lot of people would migrate outside, hanging around under a big tree up in the back parking lot or at a few picnic tables nearby. They'd smoke and stare at the ground and drink sodas and share memories and hopes until they saw Weir's silver pickup pull up again. Then they'd all hustle back down to the fire hall to hear Weir tick off the slow progress of the drill: down 40 feet; then a couple of hours or so later, down 60 feet; then 80 feet . . .

ANNETTE FOGLE:

The wait was hard on everyone. They told us eighteen hours from the time the drill started, so it was just a countdown. My daughter, Brittany, was there the whole time. She handled it very well. At one point that night, though, she did break down at the table and she cried. I asked her what was going on, and she said, "I miss my daddy. I want my daddy."

LESLIE MAYHUGH:

I'd been crying so hard on the night before, my eyes were practically swelled shut. Thursday night, I felt better. After we got back from the site, I decided Blaine was going to need something to wear when he got out from under there. So I went up to the shower house at the mine. And I asked one of the guys, "Can you please get me Blaine's clothes out?" That's all I wanted, was his clothes and shoes.

And after he gave them to me, I sat there in the truck for a few minutes and was just smelling his "The Rock" [the wrestler] T-shirt that he'd had on that day. I wanted to be close to him, you know, but I was also looking for some kind of sign, some feeling that he was trying to tell me something. Because I was sure if he was dead, I would have known it somehow. But I didn't get no signs, so that made me happy.

ANNETTE FOGLE:

I thought about a lot of things that night. I remembered back when Randy decided to go into the mines, not long after we married. The only time it scared me, him working underground, was when I was pregnant with our first child. I had had a dream one time that he had died. And that's the only time that I had been afraid and wanted him to quit.

Hopeful as she may have been, Annette was still haunted by Randy's last good-bye.

ANNETTE FOGLE:

The first night my dad showed up over there, I sat outside the fire hall with him and cried. I said, "Dad, I'm such a bonehead." He said, "No, you're not. Why do you think you're a bonehead?"

I said, "Mom told me many, many times that you don't let the sun go down on your anger. And that's what I did." I told my dad how Randy had gone to work that morning, and how I was mad at him. I said to my dad, "I kissed him, but I didn't tell him I loved him. And he turned and he looked at me." I carried that look with me, I did, all during that time.

So I said, "Dad, when Randy comes out of there, the first thing I want to say to him is that I love him. I owe him that."

13 · ROUGHING IT

THE MINERS' final redoubt was a small rectangular area about twenty feet wide by seventy feet deep at the top of entry one. Only the first thirty-five feet or so of the roof had been bolted up; the last part was unsupported, and the potential for a rock fall or cave-in was high. But this was it: the absolute highest point in this section of the mine. From here, there was no retreat.

FLATHEAD:

When we got over to entry one, it was just disbelief that we were going to die in this coal mine, you know. We just sat there for a little while in the dark. We thought, What are we going to do now? Then Randy came up with the idea of digging the loose coal out and putting canvas up to make a fake wall in front of us, so that it would sort of close us off.

Somebody had said, "Randy, that ain't going to do

much." But he said, "Well, if it holds a foot of water, that's that much more time."

HOUND DOG:

We hung a piece of canvas across the front of the entry. And we piled coal against it on the bottom and nailed it to the ribs and stuff. It was more or less psychological more than anything else, to hide the ugliness. Nobody said this at the time, but I think that's what it was. We didn't want to see the ugliness coming.

We used mine signs for shovels. All over the mine are these signs that say, DANGER—DO NOT ENTER, so nobody travels under an unsupported roof. We took them down and used them for shovels. They're just a piece of flat metal about two feet long. We laid the canvas down on the ground. Then we covered one part of it with as much coal as we could find to seal it off. Then we nailed the canvas to the ribs on each side and across the top. It was pretty tight. If the water didn't get too much pressure, maybe it would hold some back.

BOOGIE:

It reminded me of a hunting camp in there, the way we had that little area blocked off with canvas. But it served a purpose. I didn't want to see the water come up. With the canvas there, you could forget about it for a minute.

While they were putting up the canvas, several guys untied the cable from their belts so they could move around more easily. When the canvas wall was finished, everyone retied except Randy, Moe, and Harpo. They sat back to back to conserve body heat.

No one knew quite what to do next. Their predicament was just as dire as it had been at the bolter. The canvas may have blocked the water from view, but it didn't change the fact that the water was still rising fast. It was maybe thirty feet from the bottom of the entry.

Again they waited.

TUCKER:

I wanted to go climb up in the old mine somehow and take my chances with methane [a lethal gas often released in old mines]. I told Randy, "I don't care, I'm not drowning." If I could've got up in there, I'd have went in there, because you want to keep going to higher ground.

For me, the hardest thing was being there with my son-in-law. I say "son-in-law," but really Blaine is like a son to me. We're that close.

I just told him, "If anybody makes it, I hope you do. Because I've lived my fifty years." I just wanted for him to live, because to raise them two kids up without a father, I mean, it has to be terrible.

UNGER:

I thought about a lot of things. I thought about my wife and who would take care of her. I thought about my farm and how much I'd miss it. I wondered if anyone was feeding my cows, if they were being taken care of. It just all ran through my mind.

HARPO:

I saw my whole life unfold before me. I thought about my wife. I thought about my kids. And I thought about the sharpening business I run—I make custom knives. I thought, My God, how am I going to get this stuff back to these people? My brother is not going to know what to do with it, because I'm the only one that knows, and it's making me feel real bad that I have these people's stuff that I can't get back to them. And, you know, I'm just having a bad time with that.

FLATHEAD:

We had our lamps off, trying to conserve them, so it was pitch-black. We were doing a lot of silent prayer and crying. I said, "Man, I'm never going to get to go hunting with my son." And Blaine had said yeah; he said something about his boy, some more family things. And then that's when I asked John Unger if he knew the Lord's Prayer, because I didn't know it. I knowed half of it, but I didn't know it all.

UNGER:

I told him I knew it. I said the first few lines: "Our Father, who art in heaven, hallowed be thy name."

BLAINE:

When I heard them saying it, I said, "Can we all say it together?"

UNGER:

Everyone just joined in. It was just voices in the dark.

Thy kingdom come, thy will be done,
on earth as it is in heaven.
Give us this day our daily bread,
and forgive us our trespasses,
as we forgive those who trespass against us.
Lead us not into temptation
but deliver us from evil.

For thine is the kingdom,
And the power,
And the glory.
Amen.

FLATHEAD:

The prayer made me feel better. I felt a peace come over me. And at that point I wasn't afraid to die, I guess.

In the darkness, they began to lose track of time. All the guys had blue-glowing indigo watches (a favorite of coal miners, who spend all their working hours in the dark), but most of them were unsure of whether it was day or night, and the more they tried to keep track of it, the more disoriented they became. A few guys dozed off. When they woke up, they were unsure for an instant where they were or what had happened. Eventually, to be more comfortable, they untied the cable that held them together—Unger first, then the others.

By now they all understood pretty well that the pressurized air that was being blown into the mine was helping to slow the water's advance. Although they couldn't feel the rising air pressure on their bodies, they saw evidence of it around them—the plastic water jugs were pushed in, as if they were being squeezed by invisible hands.

Still, they worried. They couldn't see water now, but they could hear it, and they wondered: Was it still coming? Would it ever stop? How long would the air bubble keep it at bay? Every half hour or so, Randy got up, turned his miner's light on, pulled back the canvas, and walked down to have a look. It seemed to him that it was not coming up on them as fast as it was before, but it was hard to tell in the darkness. So he put a piece of wood held down by a rock at the water's edge.

TUCKER:

The pumps, that was the critical thing. If they just had a couple little dingy pumps going, I can tell you, it would have been all over for us. We talked about that a lot: What kinda pumps you think they got up there? How many of 'em can they run at a time? How the hell are they going to get all this water outa here?

RANDY:

I was hoping the water had flooded out into the mine entrance so they could start with the big pumps, just to get it taken care of. The guys asked me a lot of questions about it. They said, "Well, where are they going to get them big pumps at? They don't make pumps that big." I said, "It's unbelievable the pumps they make today." And they said, "Well, how are they going to get them here?" I said, "They'll fly them. Whatever it takes, they're going to get them here. They'll be here, don't worry."

Again, Randy went down to check the water. It was an hour, maybe two, after they'd finished the canvas wall.

BLAINE:

I'm sitting there, and Randy comes up through the canvas and says, "I think the water stopped rising." I said, "Don't be bullshitting me, Randy." Because at that point, I thought maybe that, his being the boss, he's trying to keep your hopes up. And he's, like, "Seriously, Blaine, it stopped." And then from there, everybody was taking turns, you know, every hour basically, every half hour, we was going to check.

BOOGIE:

I made a lot of trips down to check the water. What else was there to do? Sit in the dark. So I'd get up on my own and go check. Then I'd come back and Randy would always ask me, "How's the water, Boog?" I'd say, "About the same." It went on like that for hours. I'd come in: "How's the water, Boog?" "About the same." I'd go down again an hour later. "How's the water, Boog?" "Oh, about the same."

Then at one point it started dropping. I'd come back and say, "It went down a quarter of an inch." The guys would say, "No shit. Really, did it?" And I'd say, "Yeah, about a quarter of an inch." We thought at that time maybe we won't drown after all. And that was a hell of a good feeling.

Their elation was short-lived. The retreat of the water was so excruciatingly slow that it was hard to keep their hopes up. Okay, so maybe they wouldn't drown immediately. They still weren't going anywhere.

BLAINE:

It was around twelve hours before we noticed an inch of movement. If it's going to take this long to pump down, I'm thinking, buddy, you're talking a week and a half, two weeks or whatever. At that rate, I was afraid we were going to starve to death.

Although they had plenty of distilled water to drink, they had precious little food. Moe had some Life Savers, Flathead had a few pieces of candy. That was gone pretty quick. Even more urgent was their craving for nicotine.

Randy himself went through a few cans of snuff each day, and most of the other guys were big chewers, too. Tucker happened to have about half a can of fine-cut Skoal in the pocket of his coveralls, and that was all. They tried to stretch it out, but between nine stressed-out, nicotine-deprived men, it didn't last very long.

BLAINE:

> By now, it was, like, two days since I'd had a meal. So I started joking around a little. I said, "We're going to have to pick the weakest one to eat, you know. That's how we're gonna survive. So that means it's your big ass we're going to be eating, Randy."

Eventually fatigue took over, and they began to settle in. Several guys took their boots off and wrung out socks, then put them back on. Tucker poked a hole in his boots with a screwdriver, so every time he walked, water would squish out. Then they made a big bed for themselves out of two pieces of canvas. One piece they laid flat on the ground as a kind of rough sheet over the coal floor, the other they used as a blanket on top of them.

Randy didn't let them get too comfortable, however. Every half hour, he insisted that one of them get up and beat on a roof bolt nine times with a hammer. He knew that rescuers would be trying to detect movement underground with seismic equipment. (He was right—they were trying, but there was too much noise aboveground to hear anything.)

HOUND DOG:

We still had our hat lights, but we hardly ever turned them on. We knew we had to conserve everything we have. Guys were getting very cold. Hypothermia—that was something we were scared of. When somebody would start shivering, teeth chattering, we'd get that guy in the middle and we'd all sit around him, or he'd lay down and we'd lay on top of him.

BOOGIE:

Every time you got up, you froze. You'd just start shaking like you do out in the woods hunting when you leave a fire—teeth chattering, the whole thing. You're, like, "Boy, is it fucking cold out there. I'm fucking frozen."

TUCKER:

I'm hot-blooded. I mean, I'm always warm, no matter what. I sleep on top of the covers with the AC on. I'd go around from one guy to the other, warming them up. I'd be with one guy for a while. Then the next guy, he'd say, "Come over and warm me up, Tuck, you're the warmest little son of a bitch." I said, "Hey, boys, whatever you want, anything to survive here."

BLAINE:

When we was laying we were, like, side to side, ass to crotch. Of course, there was some joking, like, "Hey, you wanna be my wife, buddy?"

BOOGIE:

The canvas we had over us was dirty and filthy and had coal all over it. You know how you get a blanket and you snuggle up, pull it up to your chin? Oh, man, all that shit would fall down in your ears. Every time a guy beside me would move, he'd shake that stuff in my ear and eyes. I didn't like that, but there's nothing you can do about it. You just shake your head a little bit. You're just laying on the canvas. I mean, this ain't like a blanket. This is a hard piece of canvas.

RANDY:

While we were laying there, my chest was really getting to me. It was at the point where I couldn't relieve it nohow. The pain from my chest was steady all the time. It worried me a bit.

I think a lot of it was caused from me throwing

up. That oil coming out with the air really got to me. I throwed that acid up into my throat and my heart was going pretty good. That's a lot of stress to be under. I mean, when your friends are looking at you, asking questions, you've got to give them something. You don't just throw your hands up and say, "I don't know."

Yet after all their trials, the mine still had more surprises in store for them.

TUCKER:

We're all laying up there, on this piece of canvas, covered up nice and warm. We were laying like you lay beside your wife with your legs curled up, hip standing up in the air. I was sleeping. Snoring away. I'm a big snorer, I hear.

Well, the good Lord woke me up. A big piece of rock about four feet long fell out of the roof. This sucker came down and smacked me, buddy. Hit me right on the hip. And I hollered.

I said, "How in the heck could this ever happen to me?" I mean, good Lord, it's bad enough we're in here trapped and water's coming after us. Now you're going to beat me to death with a rock?

BOOGIE:

I helped Tuck lift that rock off him. Then we pounded on the ceiling with a sledgehammer to make sure no other loose bits were going to fall.

When we were done, I jumped back under the canvas. It didn't take long before our hips were sore on both sides. You have little rocks, lumps of coal digging in you. We'd all lay on our left side and put our arms around one another facing that way. If one big guy in the middle wants to move or anybody is sore and he wants to turn over, you sure got to turn over like an egg. It's pitch-dark, you know. I'd be laying there a couple times and I know the guy next to me rolled over, but I couldn't tell where his face or his head was or nothing. I just feel his breath on my cheeks.

UNGER:

When we were working in the mine, Randy always used to tell us we had to get something done or he'd kill us—like, "Hey, Unger, get that roof bolted right now or I'll kill you." It was just his way of talking. So when we were laying down there, I told him, "You really went to extremes here, Fogle. You didn't have to go this far; it would've been all right."

After years underground, the first thing a coal miner loses is his hearing. The machines they use—especially the miner—are loud, howling beasts with no sympathy for the delicate tissue of the inner ear. Of course the guys are supposed to wear earplugs, but they rarely do. Tucker had already lost 80 percent of his hearing; Moe was losing his, too.

Nevertheless, in this absolute darkness, they were dependent on their ears to tell them what was going on. Underground, the earth sounded alive, even talkative. The air pipe was no longer screaming—it was underwater now. There were groans and creaks and rumblings, weird earth-bowel sounds they had never noticed before. There were quiet hisses where the pressurized air leaked through the strata, and the insistent rhythmic clanking of a floating soda can as it bumped up against the rib of the mine.

FLATHEAD:

The air from the pipe bubbled through the water and sounded a little like an outboard motor to me. It wasn't real extreme, you could just hear it a little in the distance. And when you went down near the edge of the water, you could hear little splashes and stuff like that. It almost sounded like a lake.

BLAINE:

At one point, I don't know how many hours we'd laid there, I heard this rumbling above us. I was the first one to hear it start because my hearing is really good. And I said, "I hear the drill! They started drilling!" And a couple of the guys were, like, "No, they did not." And I said, "Listen, listen." Then Fogle heard it. He said, "Yeah, they did start."

FLATHEAD:

The water started going down, but we didn't hear anything for hours, you know. It was, like, did they give up on us or what? Then we heard the big drill and we could hear it, you know, cutting and coming. Okay, men. Everybody got positive. We knew they were coming to get us.

For the next few hours, many of the guys closed their eyes, lulled to sleep by that sweet grind of steel coming down through the earth above them.

Then it was quiet again. The distant roar of the drill was gone.

RANDY:

Hound Dog said, "What the hell happened?" I said, "Hey, either he broke a bit, or he's pulling it up to change a bit." I said, "He'll be back, don't worry, they're coming."

The minutes turned to hours, and still the grind of the drill bit did not return.

HARPO:

I just said to myself, "Dear God, please don't give up on us now."

14 · WE DROPPED THE BIT

ABOUT EVERY HOUR, John Weir made the same loop. First he'd drive down to the pit to measure how high the water that had flooded out of the mine mouth had risen; then he'd haul ass the mile or so over to the drill site to check on the progress of the rescue hole. Finally he'd rush back to the fire hall to report what he'd seen to the families. To be sure he didn't forget anything, he jotted stuff down with a pen on the insides of his arms—the number of feet the water had fallen, the number of feet the drill bit had penetrated. After a while his forearms looked like Bronx subway cars, covered with graffiti.

It was all guesswork, rough estimates. At the pit, Weir used the garage door on the maintenance shed as a kind of rough measuring stick. He knew it was eighteen feet high, and at one point the water was nearly to the top of it. As it receded, he ticked off the water level accordingly—down six inches, down a foot. At the drill site, drillers would flash him numbers with their fingers—down 50, down 60, etc.

JOHN WEIR:

Whenever I went down to the fire hall after I made my rounds, no matter what time of night, I'd see these people with their heads on the table or laying on cots. As soon as I walked in, everybody jumped up to hear what I had to say. I always thought of that commercial that's on TV of the hungry kids, all them eyeballs. And that's what I felt like the whole time, these eyeballs just staring at you and saying, Give us some hope, John, give us hope.

ANNETTE FOGLE:

I hadn't slept all of Wednesday night, all day Thursday. I didn't want to miss anything. At 2 A.M. on Friday morning, I was in the fire hall. I had laid my head on the table, thinking, Well, maybe I'll catch a few winks between. I'll be right here when they come in again.

DENISE FOY:

I was pretty worn out too. I'd been up since 6 A.M. Wednesday morning—that was going on forty-eight hours now. Leslie said, "Mom, you've got to get some sleep." I said, "I can't." I could tell she was worried about me. So she gave me some pills. She's a nurse, you know. She didn't tell me what they was. I said, "I'll take one if you take one." Well, she didn't take hers, but I took mine.

Then I went up behind the fire hall to where my sister-in-law's Blazer was parked and laid down. I went to sleep immediately.

Weir was at the site about 2 A.M. Friday, making his usual rounds. He was up by one of the barns, just bullshitting with some of the engineers. The drill rig was down to about 110 feet—almost halfway down to where the men were trapped. At this rate, they could have them out by morning.

JOHN WEIR:

All of a sudden, somebody says, "The bit broke." The drillers weren't too concerned at first; they thought they'd be able to fish it right out. But I was a little worried, because I'd never heard of anything like that happening on a rig. At first they were saying it'd be a few hours' delay.

I immediately called my wife and said, "Babe, I got bad news." She of course thought the worst. She said, "They found them." I said, "No. The damn drill bit broke. What am I going to tell these people? How am I going to break the news?" I felt like just turning around and going home. She said, "Well, just go in, it's not your fault. It's not your fault. Just go in and tell them what happened."

SUE UNGER:

John didn't even come the whole way in the fire hall. I think he came right inside the door. He was very emotional, you could see that. And he said, "I have bad news." Everybody stopped and looked at him. He said, "The drill bit broke." After that, there was complete silence in the room.

What had happened, in fact, was not unheard of when drilling in a tough spot; drillers call it "shanking the bit." The 1,500-pound bit had essentially snapped off from the upper casing that guided it into the ground. Usually it's a fairly simple matter of hooking on to the bit with a crane and yanking it out, then replacing it with a new one. If all goes well, it can be accomplished in three or four hours.

JOHN WEIR:

I tried to give them hope. I told them they'd have another one to replace it, that it wouldn't take long at all.

SUE UNGER:

Nobody knew what to say. They didn't confront him. Matter of fact, he didn't give them a chance. He said what he had to, and he was out of there because he was very emotional.

There weren't a lot of people crying in the room. We were beyond crying then.

Pretty soon, everybody started asking, "What's going to happen now?"

ANNETTE FOGLE:

The phrase I remember him using was, "We dropped the bit." It was a devastating moment. You just thought, Well, how much longer can this go on? How much more can they take?

CATHY HILEMAN:

As soon as I heard that, I went home. I didn't like to cry in front of other people. So I came home and did it on my own. I took a hot bath and got myself pulled back together.

MISSY PHILLIPPI:

I'd fallen asleep at the drill site, listening to the sound of the drill. I woke up, and I can remember thinking they were still drilling. Someone said, "Missy, it broke. The drill broke."

I said, "Well, where's the other ones?" And whoever I was talking to said, "Well, there is no other one." And I thought, Well, what the hell. And that's when I started getting mad.

Weir arrived at the fire hall a few hours later with more bad news. On a subsequent visit to the rescue site, he'd learned that not only had the drill bit broken, but it had broken in such a way that it was going to be nearly impossible to grab with the usual equipment. (Even the drillers themselves hadn't realized this at first.) To fish it out, they were going to have to fabricate a special tool to thread into a small portion of the bit, which would then give the crane something to hook on to. Still, it would be tough. This was a 1,500-pound bit, lodged 110 feet underground, covered with mud and sand. How long it might take to get it out, Weir couldn't say. Drillers who had faced this situation before knew it could be days, even weeks.

Another drilling rig was on the way, but it would be hours before it arrived and got set up.

DENISE FOY:

I was asleep in the back of the Blazer until about 5:30 A.M. As soon as I walked down to the fire hall, I could tell that something was wrong. Leslie came over and told me what happened, and we just sat down on the picnic bench out there and cried. They had been down there all these hours, and—well, it was hard not to give up hope. Tom's [Tucker's] sister came up to me and said, "I can't take this anymore, I gotta go home."

Blaine's father, Blaine Mayhugh, Sr., took the news particularly hard. "When that drill broke down, it almost killed me," he says. And he isn't speaking figuratively. Although Mr. Mayhugh doesn't look like a fragile man—he's fifty-nine, rugged, and suntanned, with rough strong hands from years working construction—he is certainly not in the best of health. A few years earlier, he'd had open heart surgery—a triple bypass. He also had high blood pressure, which tended to skyrocket in stressful situations.

At the fire hall, Mr. Mayhugh's wife, Marge, kept a close eye on him. Much to her consternation, he would often just disappear out the door. "I'd go look for him and he'd be up the road, crying," Marge recalls. "Then I'd sit down under a tree with him and we'd both be crying. He said, 'That's my best friend down there. If he dies, I might as well be dead too.'"

BLAINE MAYHUGH, SR.:

In my mind, time was of the essence. You couldn't be pissing around or whatever. But everything was too slow. Basically they was all doing one heck of a job, but I was worried. I wanted them to go down right now and get them the hell out of there.

At the time, most families focused more on the drill than on the water pumps. But in the end, it would turn out that getting the water level down was the most important thing. Because of the air bubble they'd created for the men, it would be extremely tricky to open the rescue shaft until the water had receded. So even if the bit hadn't broken, it would still have been hours before they could have tried bringing the men out.

The real trauma of the broken bit was more symbolic: It was a clear sign that things were going wrong. Even at the drilling site, the news cast a pall over everything. Red Cross workers at the food table talked quietly among themselves; engineers in shiny hard hats gathered on a bluff above the drilling rig and stared vacantly at it. Coincidentally or not, the first visible religious leader—Ed Ebersole, the pastor of a Lutheran church in nearby Duncansville—appeared on the scene, wandering around in chinos and his black collar, playing with kids and chatting with rescuers. He was a comforting, friendly, but slightly ominous presence. It was hard not to wonder if he knew something that everyone else didn't.

At the fire hall, the mood was equally dark. Counselors were available to anyone who wanted to talk. A doctor dispensed what family members called "nerve pills"—mostly Paxil, a mild antidepressant. Red Cross volunteers hovered over anyone who seemed to be having a particularly tough time, offering any help they could provide. And for the first time, someone turned the TV on in the hall, so families were able to watch live feeds from CNN and local news stations. But with the drilling halted, there wasn't much to report.

JOHN WEIR:

That afternoon, I didn't have much to tell the families, other than they were having a tool made to fish the drill bit out, and that pumps were still pumping water. It was very difficult to stand there in front of those people with nothing to say. So I started recruiting people to just come down and tell them what process was going on. We had the Navy guys talk about hypothermia and the bends, which was a risk, because of the air pressure down there. I brought some of the drillers in to talk about what was going on at the site. But basically, it was just waiting.

BLAINE MAYHUGH, SR.:

The trouble was, it seemed to me that John Weir and those other people were talking about a lot of things that weren't happening. They come in one time and told us they was going to drill other holes and they was going to send some kind of a light down, and then they told us another time they was going to send down the food and stuff through a hole. And then the next time they come back and they tell you, no, we can't do this. They'd build your hopes up, and then they wouldn't do it. It was getting me upset.

SANDY POPERNACK:

I was pretty mad about the way they were handling things. So I said to a friend, "I'd like to go clean out Mark's locker." My friend said, "He's done, isn't he?" "He's done," I said. "When he gets out, there's no way I'm letting him go back in that mine." So we went up and got his clothes and his gear, and I felt a lot better.

For the media, the lack of news was frustrating. This was rapidly becoming a global story, played out in real time, with people all over the world turning on their TVs and logging on to websites to find out whether the miners were dead or alive. Viewers wanted minute-by-minute updates and information, and the media was falling all over itself to provide it. Even Geraldo parachuted in late Friday, but rescue officials were unimpressed. "He wanted to get into the fire hall where the families were, but they turned him right around," says Weir.

Media headquarters—the parking lot of the Giant Eagle supermarket a few miles down the road from the rescue site—was a sea of satellite trucks, their dishes turned toward the sky. All day long, you could see local reporters pacing back and forth, practicing their next live stand-up or muttering to their producers on their cell phones: "They really haven't advanced the story much this afternoon. . . ."

Not surprisingly, a lot of rumors got played as news. On

Friday afternoon, John Weir happened to be talking to the families in the fire hall when a report came on live that the broken drill bit had been pulled from the rescue hole. Having just been at the site a few minutes earlier and knowing that the drill bit was nowhere close to being fished out, Weir lost his cool.

JOHN WEIR:

I looked at Barry [Ritenour, a local pastor who was helping at the fire hall], and I said, "One more false report comes over that TV and I'm going to get my .357 Magnum out of the truck and blow that son of a bitch right off a wall." I mean, I was frustrated. I was angry. The media was just making it hell for these people, spreading all this wrong information.

The next time Weir went to the fire hall, he asked Dave Rebuck of Black Wolf Coal to come with him and help explain things to the families. As it turned out, Governor Schweiker also stopped in for one of his periodic visits.

BLAINE MAYHUGH, SR.:

The governor is a hell of a nice guy, but he wasn't an authority on the stuff he was talking about. And so at some point when he and Dave Rebuck were talking, I stood up and said, "I want to know what the hell is going on. The first time you're coming in and then you tell us we're going to have the new drill here within so-and-so time, and that you're going to drill a hole and send them down some food and then you're going to send down some kind of light. And then you tell us, Well, it's going to take a little longer to get the drill and you can't really send food or a light down."

The fire hall grew silent. Unabashed, Mr. Mayhugh brought up the water pumps, which had been a topic of conversation all afternoon. Weir and others had been telling the families that they had all the water pumps they could handle—only to add a few hours later that in fact they had decided they needed even more pumps.

BLAINE MAYHUGH, SR.:

I said to the governor, "Why don't you get twenty water pumps? If you've got ten too many, who cares? Get them there and start pumping this goddamn water out and start getting the water to drop."

I was panicky. I said to the governor, "You and [Dave Rebuck] might be able to blow smoke up people's asses, but you're not going to blow smoke up my ass. There ain't no reason you don't got more water pumps."

The governor got a little hot and said to me, "I don't need to put up with talk like this."

So I said something smart—I don't remember exactly what it was. I didn't cuss, you know. The only cussword I used was "smoke up your ass."

The last thing that I said to the governor was, "I know that I am all upset, but you've got to understand that time is of the essence. You can't keep running out of options, saying you need this and then, Well, now we've got to go to West Virginia or something to get it. Where is the next place you're going to go—over to Afghanistan after a drill bit?"

While Mr. Mayhugh was carrying on, several state police officers moved in toward him, presumably afraid he might try to slug the governor. But before they got close, Mr. Mayhugh turned around and left.

BLAINE MAYHUGH, SR.:

When I got outside, I started crying. I mean, I thought I was going to lose my baby.

Then Dave Rebuck came out. I stopped him and said, "I'm sorry the way I talked, but that's my baby down there and I might never see him again." And then a couple minutes later, the governor came out and he patted me on the shoulder and said, "I understand."

I told him, "You better get my boy out of there."

He said, "We're trying to get your son and all of them out."

MARGE MAYHUGH:

As I was leaving through the back door at the fire hall, I heard this guy—I don't know who he was—say, "Who was that asshole in there?"

I said, "That asshole happens to be my husband." And then my daughter went off on him: "Unless you have a brother, a father, or a son in the mine, you have no business saying nothing." And the guy shut up now. He left and we never did see him again.

15 · VISIONS OF ACOSTA

HOUND DOG:

After that drill bit broke, we had no idea what was going on. I said, "This must be a damn union job. What do they do, drill for an hour, then go into the Ramada to drink some beer and coffee? 'That's enough for the night, let's go home. We'll start again in the morning.'" I made a joke about it, you know.

Randy said, "When we get out, you're going to be amazed by all the people that's involved with this." I said, "Well, I don't know. I just hope they soon get us out of here."

And hours turn into days. And that's when anger took over on my part, you know. Then I was getting angry. What is taking them so long?

The silence of the drill was a crushing blow to the miners' morale. In its own way, keeping faith was as exhausting as fighting raging water. And the more time that passed—

and the colder and hungrier and weaker they became—the tougher it was.

UNGER:

Hound Dog was kind of caught up, and he was driving us all a little nuts. He'd say, "I never thought I'd die this way." He said it over and over. I said, "It isn't like we planned this, you know." He was freaking, saying, "Oh, I didn't think I'd ever do this, I didn't think I was ever going to die this way." He just kept it up and kept it up and kept it up. I was, like, "What do you want me to do, hit you on the head with a rock? I mean, come on, Ron, get a grip, man. Nobody was planning on going this way."

TUCKER:

Hound Dog's mood started working on everybody. I mean, we don't have no snuff. We're getting hungry. Now the bit broke. He says, "Well, I'm getting out of here tomorrow. I'm going to go see my daughter." I say, "Well, I hate to tell you, you ain't going nowhere until they get this water pumped down, get a hole drilled, whatever. It might take a couple weeks." He says, "Well, I ain't staying here no couple weeks." I say, "You're going to stay here until whenever. You might as well just lay down, save your energy." And that's pretty much what he did.

To fill the hours, they talked about their jobs, their lot as coal miners, and why the hell they cut into the old Sax-r an mine. As it turned out, Moe knew a little bit about that old mine. His grandfather had been a mine foreman there during the 1940s. Even fifty years ago, it was known that this was a tough place to mine. "They had run into bad roofs and water," Moe says. "Conditions-wise, it was dangerous."

FLATHEAD:

I was saying, "How could this happen?" They should know that damn thing is there, you know. And then Randy said right away, "Well, them old-timers, they would steal a little extra coal here and there. And maybe the old maps weren't right." He would try scenarios, trying to explain it to us.

MOE:

My dad told me that back during the war, them mine inspectors didn't care what was going on in a mine. Money was tight. Inspectors came very seldom. The company would give inspectors a thousand bucks and say, "You don't really want to go in there and see what's going on, do you?"

BLAINE:

We were definitely angry about what happened to us. We wasn't loading good, the conditions were only getting worse. Maybe we never shoulda been down in this part of the mine to start with. Or maybe we shoulda pulled out a week or so earlier.

FLATHEAD:

When I first started with this company, it was the best thing going. I mean, everybody in Somerset County was fighting to get into this company. And they told us they wanted young men like me because they told us that we would retire from this company.

About five, six years ago, it changed. It used to be that if you put three percent into a 401(k), they'd match it. And they took that away. And it just went that way, taking away benefits, not giving us any raises, cutting vacation days, treating you worse and worse, like you're just a number, not a human being.

Unions are pretty much gone from around here. Whenever there was a vote, half the guys would go for it, and half would be against it. And they would say, "Well, if you're going to go union, we're going to shut down, you know"—use the scare tactic.

And they probably would have. They would have

closed the doors, got a new name and opened up under a new name, and rehired.

UNGER:

Last Christmas, I brought my son Stephen into the mine. He's twenty-five, you know. We rode right down to the face, right where the action is. I told him, "Come on, bud. This is where it's at." Well, he only stayed an hour. I had to take him out. He said, "Nobody in their right mind would make a living this way."

Late in the day on Friday, Randy and the crew got an unexpected gift. Tucker, who had been lying down for quite a while, his chest hurting, now decided it was time to get up and do some exploring.

TUCKER:

I remembered the other day there we went up to this bolter and they had, like, four or five bottles of Mountain Dew and I just throwed them all away because we want to get this cleaned up because I know the inspector is coming in the next day. I figured that might get me in trouble.

Anyhow, I figured I'm going to see if there's anything on that bolter I can find. So I went up there. I seen this bottle of Mountain Dew setting right beside this dust box. So I pulled it out, and there was another one, and also a full bottle of Sierra Mist.

So I took that back and we all drank. Then I kept sniffing around for more. I went down in this crosscut and I seen Harpo's bucket floating around. I figured it was probably empty, or full of mud. I opened that sucker up, and honest to God, buddy, it was just as dry as could be in there. There was a corned beef sandwich and a full can of Pepsi. I just wished there was a can of snuff in there. Them guys would have given me a big kiss for that.

The sandwich was nice and lifted their spirits momentarily (although the sodas and sandwich ended up giving several guys a bad case of indigestion). But one bite of a sandwich, they knew, was not going to make the difference in whether they survived or not. At this point, their lamps were getting dim, and they worried that soon the only lights would be their Indiglo watches. The cold was seeping into their bones, and it was harder and harder to keep their morale up.

BOOGIE:

We were hitting the bolt every half hour. But toward the end, nobody even wanted to get up and hit the bolt. It was just so damn cold when you got up. We didn't even want to get up to piss.

I would only doze off ten minutes at a time. I'm not

a sleeper to start with. I'd doze off for ten minutes at the most, but then I'd be up for hours. But I liked laying down for the heat.

I'd say, "Hey, somebody's got to get up and hit the bolt nine times." Nobody would answer. So I'd get up. I didn't want to either, but I did. It was something I was trying to take care of. I'd turn my light on and crawl out from under them guys, bang nine times with the sledge, drop it, crawl back in, turn my light out, and snuggle right back up.

FLATHEAD:

I just laid there. Randy yelled at me a couple times and made me go down and beat on the roof just to make me move. I was tired, I was depressed, I didn't care no more and I just didn't want to do anything. I just didn't care anymore.

Randy would say, "Get your ass up, Flathead, it's your turn." And he had to tell me that two or three times before I'd go.

BOOGIE:

Everyone knew Randy was hurting. I mean, he didn't move. We'd ask him, "You okay, Randy?" "Yeah, I'm okay," he'd say.

We were worried about him.

In fact, the darkness, the quiet, and the isolation was starting to get to all of them.

MOE:

I think me and Blaine probably slept less than anyone. We were just sitting there back to back and . . . I mean, we've never seen this dark of a place, as dark as it gets. But this light kept coming up to the right side of my head. It was like a streak.

BLAINE:

Moe goes, "Did you see that bright light?" I'm, like, "Yeah, off to my right." We both was looking at the exact same thing.

HOUND DOG:

They made fun of us there. But my right hand to God, something was down there. I could see light down there.

It was a glow, like a light just around the corner. Like if you have a light around the corner of the house and you see the glow, that's what I seen.

BOOGIE:

I did a lot of staring into the dark. I couldn't sleep. I'd doze off ten minutes here and there. And at one point

Hound Dog says, "I can see my feet." I said, "I'll tell you what, I can see my feet, too."

UNGER:

They asked me what I saw, and I told them, "A lot of black, man." They said, "Don't you see that light up there?" I said no. I don't know what it was, but I think it's the way your eyes adjust to the darkness.

I said, "This isn't the sixties, man. I don't know. I'm missing it here." They all started laughing. "What are you on, man? Whatever it is, I need some."

BOOGIE:

A little later, I was sitting back to back with Hound Dog. I was staring in the dark. And I seen something. I'll tell you exactly what I seen. I'm not crazy.

I felt like I was sitting on a hill. I told Hound Dog about it. I said, "Hound Dog, what I see right now—it's a full moon. I'm looking at a town. The stars are all out. A beautiful sky with stars and a full moon. I can see a row of houses to my right and a row of houses, like company houses, to my left. I can see a row of treetops behind the houses. I can see it."

The town looked to me a little bit like Acosta [an old coal mining town nearby]. The more I stared, the better it really looked. I didn't see no ghosts or anything.

I seen this town. It was a pretty town. The sky was beautiful with stars.

Unger said, "You guys are nuts. You're losing it."

And I said to John, "I ain't nuts. I'm just telling you what I see."

16 · THE LONGEST DAY

O N FRIDAY NIGHT, Governor Schweiker had predicted that one of the drills would complete the 245-foot shaft and break through to the miners by early Saturday morning. Like many of the governor's predictions, that turned out to be a little too optimistic. At 6 A.M. on Saturday, Duane Yost, the driller in charge of the rig on rescue hole number one, was at about 130 feet. Larry Winckler, the driller in charge of the rig on rescue hole number two, was at about 145 feet.

Given his late start, Winckler thought he was doing pretty well. The rig had come in from North Canton, Ohio, on Thursday afternoon, and had already popped down a 290-foot dewatering hole in a field about a half mile from the main rescue site. Winckler's crew was getting ready to drill another dewatering hole on Friday morning when David Hess of the Pennsylvania DEP (Department of Environmental Protection) told them to move their rig over to the rescue site—the bit in rescue hole one was stuck, and they wanted to get another hole going right away.

So Winckler broke down the rig and moved over to the main rescue site, which was so jammed with people and equipment that it was, as Winckler puts it, "all asses and elbows." Engineers directed Winckler's rig to a spot about 75 feet from rescue hole number one. Winckler finally got the compressors and everything else he needed in place, and was drilling by about 6 P.M. on Friday. By 7 P.M., he was already down 45 feet.

Over at rescue hole number one, Duane Yost was having his own troubles. After having a special tool fashioned at a local shop, the crew was finally able to hook the bit and haul it out at about 5 P.M. on Friday. Yost threw on another 30-inch bit, but for some reason it wasn't cutting correctly. He spent a few hours getting nowhere, then pulled it out—an hour-long process—and switched to a smaller 26-inch bit. That went much faster. But it was a bit of a risk, too: If the shaft wasn't perfectly straight, they'd have a hell of a time getting the 22-inch rescue capsule down there.

Yost and Winckler couldn't help but feel like they were in a race against time—and each other. They both were running nearly identical Ingersoll-Rand drilling rigs that cost about a million bucks apiece, and both were manned by four-man crews round the clock. They wanted nothing more than to see these nine miners lifted safely out of the ground, but professional pride was also at stake here.

Winckler was at a slight disadvantage because his hole was bigger, a full 30 inches across. He had been drilling all night long, and after hitting a rough patch of limestone at about 100 feet, he was making good progress by the time Governor Schweiker came by for his early morning briefing. Still, he was nowhere near fulfilling the governor's prediction of reaching the miners by dawn. Knowing that he was going to face some tough questions at the fire hall, Governor Schweiker asked Winckler to come along and talk to the families with him.

LARRY WINCKLER:

We got to the fire hall at about 6 A.M. I was very tired and had been working very hard and wasn't looking forward to this. But the governor asked, so I went. I could see right away that people were real concerned. It was pretty emotional. We all knew we were running out of time. But I just tried to explain to the families exactly what we were doing, and why it takes so long to drill these holes—drilling a 30-inch hole is not like drilling a 6-inch hole, you know. It's just a very tricky operation. And we were running into some limestone, which slowed things down. I said to them, "You just have to be patient. There is nothing I can do to speed this up. If we try to rush, we're going to have problems." They understood that, but, you know, it was tough. It was very tough. We all knew we were reaching the point of no return for these guys. We had to get them out.

For the families in the fire hall, patience was a luxury they could not afford. They knew if Randy and his crew were not out of the mine in the next twelve hours or so, chances were exceedingly slim that they would ever see them alive again.

ANNETTE FOGLE:

At first, you heard it was only going to be a matter of hours, or else you heard it would be eighteen hours. Like Thursday, it was eighteen hours. So you figured Friday at the latest. And then you thought Saturday morning at the latest. Well, Saturday morning came and went, and it didn't happen. Then they would come in and say it's a couple more hours. And it just went on and on. So you got to the point where you wondered if when they got down there, if it was going to be in time and what they were going to find.

Luckily, I have a wonderful family that kept me going. And there had been an article in the newspaper about some other miners who'd been trapped under-ground for seven days. So I thought, If they can do it, these guys can do it. Randy had told me many times he had a good crew, and they had a lot of experience between them. So I was still hopeful.

Then again, maybe I was just hoping he would come out so I could tell him that I loved him. That's the one thing I wanted. Those were the first words I wanted to say to him.

Except for the pounding of the drills, and the small team of big busy men swarming around them, the rescue site was oddly serene on Saturday morning. A silvery mist rose off the green hay fields surrounding the rescue site, and out along the dirt road that led to the rear of the site, a herd of cows chewed their cud. Groggy rescuers rolled out of the backseats of their pickup trucks, stumbling over to the food table in the barn for hot coffee. Doug Custer was out there fairly early, looking red-eyed and shaggy from lack of sleep.

At the coffeepot, there was quiet disappointment about the lack of progress on the drill holes, but it was masked by a lot of talk about numbers—"I just heard rig one is at 150." "Just talked to the driller on two, he's at 145." "Any-body heard about how the pumpin' is going out back?" "I heard the water's down to 1833." This kind of talk was not just a way of marking progress, it was also a way of avoiding the one question everyone dreaded: Was there any way these guys could possibly still be alive?

Everyone knew the water pumps were the key to the rescue—the only way to get them out safely and quickly was to get the water down. But the drillers were the stars. All day Saturday, a crowd of engineers, volunteers, and rescue workers sat on the bluff above the site, staring down at them with a certain kind of awe. Watching these guys work, mud splattering all over them, refusing to break for longer than it took to chug a bottle of fruit punch POWERade (the drink of choice at the rescue site), it was impossible not to think of the ironworkers, firemen, and police officers who had dug through the rubble at the World Trade Center. Once again, lives depended on big muscle and big iron. And these guys—with their T-shirts, tattoos, lips wadded with chew—were about as tough as they came.

LESLIE MAYHUGH:

Saturday morning, John Weir took some families around so we could see things for ourselves. My cousin David and I went on one of those trips. First we went down to the pit and I seen how much water there was. By then it was pretty much pumped out, but I could see the marks where the high water had been. And they showed me the big pumps. Then they took me down to the drill site, where we saw the two drills working. I walked right up to the drill rig and said, "Let me see how big this hole is." I couldn't imagine my dad and my husband coming out of a 26-inch hole. I was thinking that they were going to get down there and then they were not going to fit. I mean, Blaine wears 36-inch pants. How was he going to fit through a 26-inch hole? I mean, I wasn't thinking [Leslie was confusing circumference—how jeans are measured—with diameter—how the rescue hole was measured].

I walked up, and stuff was splashing—there was a lot of water and mud. I looked down into the hole, and I'm like, "All right, they can get out. It's big enough." That's one worry I had. But when I'm there, I'm in this daze—I can't believe I'm standing right on top of my husband and my dad.

One of the guys on the drill rig, Brandon Fisher, happened to be a year ahead of me in school. And he turned around and he saw me. He just said, "Is Blaine down there?" I said, "Yes, and my dad." Somehow, he already knew my dad was down there. And he knew I married a guy from Meyersdale that worked in the mine, but he didn't know they were on the same crew.

And then Brandon just took his hat off and started sobbing.

I said, "You just get him out, okay? Just get him out."

In the early afternoon, Winckler noticed his drill was slowing down. Normally, he would have pulled the bit up and checked it. But he was desperate to reach the trapped miners, so he pushed on. At about 3 P.M., when he was down about 200 feet—only 40 feet to go—he noticed the air pressure dropping on his rig. "It was clear that it wasn't cutting," he says. But he wasn't sure why. He decided to pull the bit up—an exhausting procedure that wasted another precious hour. As the end of the drilling pipe came into view, he saw the problem—the bit was gone. It had snapped off.

JOHN WEIR:

I'd say that Larry Winckler is a man of the fewest words I've ever run into. During all this, he never spoke to me. He just gave me fingers all the time, how far they were down. That was how he communicated. He's a no-nonsense guy, just wants to get the job done, and doesn't waste words talking about it.

When that drill bit broke, he grabbed me and gave me a big squeeze. And Larry, you know, he's a big guy.

He was holding me so tight, I thought my eyeballs were going to pop out. And he is just bawling. Now, I lost it too. I looked around at all these guys on the rig, guys who are filthy, eyes red for working so long, guys who are tough as nails and probably take the beer caps off with their teeth, they're all in tears because they thought they let us down. But I told him, "Larry, you didn't." He gave us what we needed to tell them people. He gave us feet, inches, when we really needed them.

For the families, the constant up and down of hope and despair was wearing them out. In a way, their situation was worse than that of their husbands and sons trapped underground—at least Randy and his crew knew they were alive. For the families, it had been a four-day-long roller-coaster ride of desperate emotion, and some of them were ready to just jump off.

MARGE MAYHUGH:

I went to the site on Saturday for a visit, and I totally lost it. I came back to the fire hall and all I remember saying is, "My son is dead, you'll bring him up dead and I might as well be dead, too."

If it wouldn't have been for my grandson, I probably would have taken a bottle of pills. It was at that point. I went and got a bottle and I had intentions of swallowing them.

My grandson David made sure I only took the one pill and went over and sat in the grass and he put his arm around me. He said, "Grandma, they'll bring him up. They'll bring him up." I just couldn't get it through my head he was coming up. Not alive, anyhow.

CATHY HILEMAN:

On Saturday, I decided that no matter what happened, Ron [Hound Dog] wasn't going back into the mine. So I asked if I could go up and clean his locker out and get his truck. I don't even know who I asked, but they said, "Well, you're not allowed up there." I said, "It's my husband's stuff and I want it." So I talked to one of the preachers. He said, "If that's what you want, I'll go and talk to them."

So I went up to the mine and I asked for Ron's wallet and other things. And the guy there said, "Okay, I'll go get his wallet for you." I said, "No, just bring everything out. He's not coming back here to work." He said, "He's going to be okay, Cathy." I said, "I just want everything."

LESLIE MAYHUGH:

Late Saturday afternoon, I talked to my preacher about services for Blaine and my father. I said, "I'm telling you now, while I'm in my right state of mind, do both of them together, a double funeral. If they die together, they're going to be buried together." And I said, "We're going to celebrate. We're going to celebrate Blaine and we're going to celebrate Dad."

At this point, it had just been going on too long. My preacher told me to just keep praying. I said, "I've been doing that. Can you tell me they're going to come out alive?" And he couldn't. So I said, "Well, I'm getting plans ready because if it happens, I'm afraid I'm going to lose it, and I don't want to worry about arrangements. I want to just take care of my kids."

By Saturday, Missy was the only family member still at the rescue site. The only two who stayed beyond the trips organized by John Weir had been Sandy and Missy, and Saturday morning, Sandy went home to take a shower. But Missy refused to budge. She borrowed a camouflage military jacket from one of the Navy guys and spent much of the day pacing behind the barns with Doug Custer, both of them looking like they were on the verge of emotional collapse.

MISSY PHILLIPPI:

Some time in the afternoon, me and a friend went over to the barn to get some food. I had two pieces of pizza and a drink and a bag of chips. We went past a guy from the DEP, and my friend knew him and we stopped to chat. I was standing a little ways away and wasn't really listening, but then I heard something that caught my attention. He said, "Time is not our friend here."

I said, "What do you mean?" And he said something about they missed getting them out two times. I don't know what he meant by that and to this day, I still don't. But he said it quite clearly and I looked at him. I was holding that plate and I sat it down on the chair and I said, "What are you trying to tell me? Are you trying to tell me something, that they missed twice getting them out and now you think that they're dead?"

He just stared at me.

Well, I knew time was running out, but I didn't realize that they thought that they were dead by then.

At about that time, I noticed Governor Schweiker over at the big blue truck they were using as a command center. I started storming over to Schweiker. My friend grabbed me by the arm and he said, "Missy, stay here, you're not going to get nowhere if you go up to the governor and start cussing like a sailor."

I said, "Well, what was that guy trying to say? They all think they're dead, don't they?"

Then I heard the state troopers saying something about body bags. And I don't know if they were preparing themselves for the worst or what. But at that point, I was flipping out pretty good.

On Saturday, the U.S. Navy was visibly present at the rescue site. They were, after all, experts in underwater rescue. They had trucked in nine hyperbaric chambers, or depressurization tanks, in case any of the miners were to get the bends from a sudden change in the pressure in the mine. The portable chambers were lined up in the barn, right next to tractors and other farm equipment, and looked like small blue space capsules. Behind the barn were several larger chambers, which took up the entire length of a flatbed truck trailer. Although their presence was welcome, and added an air of seriousness to the rescue operations, the naval officers looked oddly out of place amidst the drills, cornfields, and cows. They were dressed in sparkling white uniforms at a place where the real badge of honor was dust and mud.

MISSY PHILLIPPI:

At about 8 P.M., I walked back behind the building where the Navy was set up and there was the master chief [the top Navy officer at the scene]. He was in his dress uniform and everything. I went up to him and I said, "Just what do you know about what the hell is going on around here now, Master Chief?" I did call him Master Chief, like that mattered. And he said, "What do you mean?" And I said, "Well, from what I hear, my husband is dead. They missed two chances and now he's dead."

Well, the master chief started getting facial twitches. He wears glasses, and his glasses were moving. He said, "Oh, I don't know. I'm getting ready to go talk to Geraldo and do an interview with him. You'll have to excuse me."

I said, "Oh, you are, are you? Why don't you give me a ride, because I'm going up to the media center, too," I told him, "because I'm going to tell the whole United States that this big shot rescue team killed our husbands because they missed two chances and now they think they're fucking dead."

He was twitching. I never seen anything like it. I'm thinking, Missy, stop it, but, you know, I couldn't. And he said, "Well, I don't rightly know about that stuff." And I'm, like, "Well, I'm telling you what, if my husband's dead, if they missed it or screwed it up, they're going to fucking pay."

And I walked away. I went and found a cot behind one of them decompression chambers. I took an old blanket and covered myself the whole way up because I couldn't take it no more. This was a little after 8 P.M., I think, when I fell asleep.

17 · WHO WANTS TO GO HOME?

HOUND DOG:

I couldn't take no more laying on that hard bottom. My hips and stuff was so sore and my back was hurting me and my feet was hurting me and everything. I said, "If I got to spend one more night in here, I'm going to lose it." This is it. I can't take no more. I'm getting out of here one way or another. What the hell is taking them so long? I just can't understand it. I mean, I was getting angry.

BOOGIE:

He was bitching. Well, what are you going to do, Hound Dog? Then Harpo starts talking about how his boys this weekend are going to a hunting safety course, both of them. They're twelve years, thirteen years old. He said, "I ain't going to get to see my boys hunt." I said, "Yeah." And I'm thinking, there's a lot of personal things to think about not seeing the family. I got a nice long-bearded turkey this year. I'm thinking, that's my last bird. At least I'll die when I'm fifty years old. At least I got to see my family graduate and on their own, which I always wanted to live to see—my kids graduate from high school—and I done that. I'm fifty years old. I was sort of trying to cheer myself up in that category. And there's Blaine. Blaine was quiet a long time.

UNGER:

On Saturday, Hound Dog went over the edge. He was going on—"I can't take another goddamn day and this is bullshit, this is bullshit." I said, "Well, what do you got planned? I don't see nothing coming in here to get us, you know."

HOUND DOG:

The other guys were telling me to calm down. You know, they're doing the best they can. They're doing this, they're doing that. Okay. But I just still can't understand what's taking them so long. You know, they're just drilling a hole. It don't take that long to drill a hole. I'm not a driller, but I could drill a hole faster than this.

I had no idea what they were doing. I mean, I just didn't know if they were up there dicking around. I just couldn't understand why it was taking so long to drill a damn hole down through the ground.

UNGER:

I told Hound Dog, "It doesn't matter how much bullshit there is, we can't go anywhere until they come. Unless you got a big plan here, it doesn't look like we're walking out. The only thing we can do is wait."

BLAINE:

When Hound Dog was ranting, I told Randy, "Another day of this and I'm going to kill him." Which was just a joke, but he was driving me nuts. I mean, it was nothing against him. He's a good guy. It's just his mind, he couldn't handle it no more.

HARPO:

I knew what Hound Dog was feeling. I think we all did. You know, I'd had enough. My light was probably the best out of all of them, and I thought about going over into the old mine where the water come out and I was going to venture around, turn my light out and just look for a speck of light from somewhere. I was going to dig my way out of there because I was not spending another night in there. I mean, I couldn't take it.

For Harpo, Saturday was pure hell. Not only was he cold, wet, tired, hungry, scared, death-addled, and nicotine-deprived. Saturday also happened to be his son Derek's twelfth birthday.

HARPO:

It's Derek's birthday, and I'm down here. I thought I might never see him again. I thought about all the things I should have done with my two boys that I didn't have time to do, you know, because I was working all the time, and not spending as much time with my family as I should have.

Still, Unger was right—there was nothing they could do but wait. So that's what they did. Flathead slept. Randy worried about his heart. Blaine did push-ups (thirty of them). Unger rubbed his shoulder, which, for some reason, was starting to ache badly. They wondered aloud if the guys at the other end of the mine had gotten out safely. They talked about sex, and wondered if they would ever have it again. They talked about hunting, and they remembered the big fish that got away. And they talked about life, and how grateful and good they would be if they ever got out of there alive.

UNGER:

To keep our spirits up, we talked about what we were going to do when we got out. We made plans, you know. Nobody had anything extravagant in mind. Harpo was going to have a cigarette and a beer and a chew. The cigarette first and then the beer and then the chew, I think was the order he was going to do stuff. I figured I was going to take a shower and go home and kick back and maybe pour myself a shot or something, you know, to kind of ease the tension, kind of unwind things.

TUCKER:

I went down by the feeder, it has this little ledge on it like that where the coal car dumps. There was a little bit of coal there and I just routed that out, cut me a piece of canvas, then went up to the bolter and got me an air filter. I took my hammer and bent it down in there a little bit, made like a lounge chair. I just laid back there, buddy. I'd lay there for a couple hours, just waiting and listening.

At about 2:30 P.M., Yost's drill finally reached a depth of about 230 feet, roughly 15 feet above the floor of the mine. For the next five hours, he shut the drill down. The water level was still a few feet above the magic elevation of 1,829 feet, which was the level at which rescue officials decided they needed to be before they could safely open the hole into the mine. "The water was going down about six inches per hour," Yost says. "There was nothing to do but wait it out."

Meanwhile, night had fallen, and under the bright floodlights, the rescue site took on a movie-set glow. On the hill above the drill hole, the Sipesville Volunteer Fire Department was running through a last-minute rehearsal of how they were going to carry the men—dead or alive—up the hill to the medical staging area. Behind the barns, a long row of ambulances prepared to whisk the men off to hospitals in nearby Johnstown and Somerset.

At about 8:30 P.M., Yost started drilling again. He took it very slowly, going down only a foot or two, then stopping the bit, blowing air and water through the hole to clear out the cuttings, then drilling another foot or two. Yost was afraid that if he didn't keep the hole clean, the bit might break through the roof of the mine and then get wedged in the shaft (it happens), rendering it useless to rescue the men. "At the end, I was going down six inches at a time, taking it real slow," Yost recalls. The crew kept their eyes on the air pressure readings and the hydraulic gauge that show the amount of weight on the drill bit. When both gauges dropped, Yost knew he had broken through to the mine.

At the rescue site, this was the moment of truth. After almost four days of roaring heavy equipment and chaos, everything was suddenly silent and still. They shut down all the air compressors, the drill rigs, the nearby water pumps. Rob Zaremski, who works for a Pennsylvania manufacturer of industrial safety equipment, prepared to lower a slender little audio device—it looked like a microphone but could both pick up and broadcast sounds, similar to a speaker-phone—into the hole to check for signs of life. To make sure the miners could see it, they taped two glow sticks to the probe—one pink, and one purple.

BOOGIE:

Suddenly, the air quit. It was the loudest thing in the mine, and it quit.

And I said, "Hound Dog, go down there and tap on that pipe. Maybe somebody would happen to be going by the pipe." This is how we were thinking, like nobody's up there. Hopefully somebody might happen to be going by and they might hear it, is what I'm thinking. He said, "I'm going down." And Tucker got up and said, "I'll go with you, Hound Dog."

HOUND DOG:

So Tucker and I got up and went down to the air shaft. And they had cut the air, they shut it off. It was dead quiet now.

Tucker and I looked at each other. What's going on? I thought they gave up.

I said, "Tuck, bang on that pipe." So he hammered on the pipe nine times. And we put our hands against the drill bit to see if we could feel any vibration coming back. You couldn't actually hear them pounding on it up there, but you could feel it. And we felt them tap back.

And just about that quick, zip, there it goes. They pulled the bit back up through the hole.

We're sitting there looking—it's gone. It's gone. It ain't there no more. I'm like, "What the hell is going on? They must be quitting." They took the air, they took the air shaft, they took the drill, they took everything. It was all gone.

After they pulled it up, we're standing there a minute and you could hear pipes banging up there, like they were taking the drill apart and throwing them on a pile. So I said to Tucker, "Shine your light up that hole and see what you can see up there." So he did. He's got his hat off—his light off his hat. And he's looking. I say, "Do you see anything?" "No, I can't see nothing."

Standing a few feet back from the rescue hole, wearing mud-splattered jeans and a bright yellow hard hat, Zaremski clamped on a set of headphones and listened. A team of men slowly lowered the probe into the 6-inch air shaft.

Zaremski called out, over and over, the words that the deep mine rescue team had told him to use: "Can you hear me? Stay where you are." Then a few seconds later: "Can you hear me? Stay where you are."

Zaremski listened, trying to block out aboveground noise and concentrate on the sounds coming out of the mine itself.

HOUND DOG:

I heard a hissing noise down there. It was coming through some of the cracks in the walls. I didn't know what it was. I said to Tuck, "Is that air coming through that wall or what?" He said, "I don't hear nothing."

He's still looking up through that air hole, trying to shine his light up there.

He's hollering, "Hey. Ho. Hey up there. Anybody up there?"

I thought, "I'm going down and figure out why that

wall is hissing. Is there that much air pushing out behind that wall or what?"

So I took my hammer down and I started knocking that top block out. And I got the top block knocked out and I looked through. As soon as I looked through, the water was just gushing out of that hole, the 30-inch hole that they drilled. The water was just pouring out in buckets; probably underground streams that they were drilling through.

Tucker said, "I'll be damned." So he come running. He looked through and said, "There's the hole." He went ahead and started tearing more of the wall out so we could get through. And I said, "Well, I'm going up to get the guys." So I walked up and poked my head through the canvas. Everybody's still sacked out.

I said, "Hey, who wants to go home?"

BOOGIE:

When he said that, we were like, "No fucking way. No shit? Get out, man." We jumped up. "Let's go! God, let's go!"

JOHN WEIR:

I wish I had a picture of [Rob Zaremski's] face when he dropped that probe down there. It was dead silent at the site and he was concentrating really hard. When he heard those voices down there, his eyes just popped out of his head.

As soon as he flashed us a thumbs-up, I was out of there. I wanted to get to the fire hall and tell the families and make sure they were the first to know.

18 · BORN AGAIN

SANDY POPERNACK:

On Saturday evening, they told me it would be midnight until they actually broke through. Everybody said, "Why don't you go home and get cleaned up, take the boys." I brought the boys home with me and they got their baths. I was brushing their teeth and the phone rang and my dad said, "They're just getting ready to break through, I'm going to come out and pick you up." I said, "No, no, I'll drive in." And he said, "No, I'm going to come and pick you up."

I was nervous. I was psyched that he was fine, but in the back of my mind, I thought, "Oh, God, how are they going to find these guys, what condition are they going to be in?" I was in tears at that point. I was scared. I was brushing my son Dan's teeth, and he started crying. He said, "I just want Dad."

I said, "We're going to get him right now, we're going to get Daddy."

JOHN WEIR:

After we got the thumbs-up from Rob, Dave Rebuck and I hopped in the back of a police car. Out of all the state cops I know here, we got a rookie. As we were leaving the drill site, he actually said to me, "Which way do I turn?" He had no idea where the fire hall was or nothing. I told him to take a right, and he just stepped on it. We musta hit 100 m.p.h.—I'm not in a seat belt, and I always wear a seat belt. Dave is sitting in the backseat, the siren is on. And I said, "Hey, buddy, you got a double S-turn down here, slow this thing down. I don't want to die to go tell these people this." There was two drill rigs sitting down on the edge of Route 985 right down along there, and I thought we were going to kiss one of them rigs as we went flying by.

When we got to the turn for the fire hall, I said, "Right here, make a right." When he made the right, I'll tell you, his ass end was sliding. When she got straightened out, he pushed that sucker to the floor, not knowing the fire hall was just a hundred yards or so ahead. And there's a little knoll—when he hit it, all four wheels was off the ground. We arrived with the sirens on, and people were already running toward the fire hall. We skidded in there and jumped out.

SANDY POPERNACK:

Dad came and the preacher came with him, and then we no sooner pulled into the fire hall than everybody came flying up to me. They said, "Get in there, get in there fast, they've got something they've got to tell you guys."

I said, "What's going on?" And I lost it again. I said, "I can't do this anymore." I hyperventilated. My dad pushed me into the fire hall. Dan said he wanted to sleep in the car, so I left him behind there.

The families gathered around Weir, waiting for the news. After having gone through so much in the last seventy-seven hours, many of them could now read Weir like a book—they knew by the look on his face that he was not bringing bad news. But they did not dare let themselves believe it until they heard him say the words.

JOHN WEIR:

I said to the families, "Listen, I've been truthful with you people, you've got to make me one promise—you can't leave the fire hall. You've got to stay here until we get them out." Because, you know, they were worried that there was going to be a stampede down to the rescue site.

Then I said, "We've got nine alive!" And the place went nuts.

ANNETTE FOGLE:

When that news came, it was cloud nine. And that fire hall, oh, man—it was shifting on its foundation, there was so much rocking and rolling. I mean people were hugging people they never knew before. Let me tell you, you didn't care who you grabbed and hugged. It was unreal.

Outside, some of the wives were crying, but not me. I said, "Turn on your radio, I want to dance." Then I decided, heck, I didn't need any music. I'm just going to dance.

SANDY POPERNACK:

I gave a sigh of relief. Everybody was just—I mean, my dad was crying. I probably cried harder knowing my dad was crying. I can't tell you when I last had a hug from my dad, but it was a good feeling.

And poor Dan, you know. He had got out of the car during the stampede of everybody running in and he couldn't get in, he was being pushed. They were almost knocking him down. But when he got in there, I grabbed him and hugged him and said, "Daddy is okay, Daddy is okay."

BLAINE, SR.:

I was hugging and kissing people I never seen in my life. And then I went up to the governor and hugged him.

MISSY PHILLIPPI:

I was still asleep at the site when this guy from the Navy, Doug Bennett, a super nice human being, jerked me up off that cot. He said, "Missy, they're alive." I remember it was 10:29 P.M. because I had ahold of his arm and I looked at his watch. I said, "Are you sure?" And he's hugging me, he's, like, "Yes, yes!"

Underground, the joy and chaos and confusion mirrored what was happening in the fire hall.

BOOGIE:

Most of us couldn't see, it was so damn dark, and our lights were almost burned out. We all beat it on down to this hole. Hound Dog took us down, you know. We're looking through this hole, and the water is just pouring out. I said, "That's it, fellows, that's where we're getting out." Then all of a sudden here comes this doggone thing down through the 6-inch. We're, like, "What the hell's that?" That scared the hell out of me. It had two big pink and purple glow sticks attached to it. It's a damn telephone.

FLATHEAD:

I grabbed it. It wasn't exactly a telephone—I think they called it a probe. It was laying in the mud and I picked it up and I said, "Hello, hello, anybody there?" And then all of a sudden, it started crackling, and then this fellow said his name and said he was with the rescue team. He asked how we was doing, and the condition of everybody. I told him we had Randy with heart trouble and John with his shoulder and I think Tucker with his heart. And they wanted me to describe the area of the hole where the shaft came through to make sure the cage would fit. And he asked me, "Is there anything you want to know?" I said, "Yeah, is our families up there?" and he said they were at the fire hall. Then I asked about the other guys, if they had made it out. Because the whole time this was going on we was worried about the other guys down below. We thought, "Man, I don't know if they made it." But he said, "Yeah, they made it out." And I told the other guys who were down there with me, and they were yelling, "Great!" and we were all happy, really happy. That was a high point, a real high point.

Then the guy asked, "Is there anything you want?" I said, "Yeah, some snuff and food." And then somebody yelled "Beer!" and I said, "Yeah, send some beer down too." But of course they wouldn't do that.

Then I had to give Randy's weight and height and description and all that. And he told me that since Randy's the biggest one and the one that was hurt, he should come up first. And he said, "Don't tell him he's going because he's hurt, tell him he's the biggest man and the biggest man has to go first." So that's what I said.

HOUND DOG:

They sent down wool blankets and flashlights and some hat lights and candy bars and water and snuff. We unloaded it out of the cage there and spread it out there, not too far from the cage, but back a ways. And we got into everything. Brand new wool Army blankets. They were in plastic. Boy, them things was nice. I opened one up and wrapped it around me. I said to Boog, "Boy, I'm going to take one of these. I'm going to sneak it out when I get up there." So Boog grabbed one and wrapped it around him and said, "Yeah, they are nice."

They shipped down some raincoats, too, and I put one on. My light was real dim, almost dead, so I grabbed a flashlight. I took a chew of snuff and then I got a drink of water and ate a candy bar. It all happened a little too fast, and I didn't feel good.

BOOGIE:

At first, they couldn't get that damn rescue capsule to come down. It took like three or four tries and it's stuck. We're thinking, "What's next? They can't get the thing down?" We don't even know what it looks like. Somebody said, "We'll send instructions down how to get in." I thought, No, I'm not going to read no instructions. We'll figure it out.

So we're waiting for this damn thing to come down. I looked at Harpo and Hound Dog and said, "I'll tell you what, guys. When we get out of here, I ain't going to no hospital. When we get up there, somebody's got to have a pickup truck around. We'll jump in the back and get a ride over to the fire hall, where our families are at." That's what we were thinking. Like we'll just get a ride home in a pickup truck.

Hound Dog said, "Do you think anybody will be there for you, Boog?" I said, "I don't know, it's pretty late. Hell, it's after midnight." I said, "I don't know if Cindy will be up this late or not. And my parents are probably in bed. You know, they go to bed early. So I don't know if anybody's going to be there for me or not. Maybe not."

Then Harpo said, "I ain't going to no hospital either. We'll get on back of a pickup truck, we'll go get a shower, we'll go over to the fire hall and see who's there." So that was our plan.

UNGER:

They finally got the capsule down and we told them we wanted to send Fogle first—except he didn't want to go. "Tell you what we're going to do," I told Fogle, "we're going to send your fat ass up there first. If you get stuck up in there and they drop you back down, I'm hitting you in the head with a rock and rolling you out of the way." And I told him, "We ain't messing around now, so you better get this thing up there. We want out of here. We don't have time to be bullshitting around here, man."

RANDY:

I didn't want to go first—that wasn't the deal, you know. But they were all pretty persuasive, so I got in that cage. It was a tight fit, there was water pouring down. I put the headphones on and they started to haul it up. They were talking to you all the way. I heard the guy say, "You're at 150 feet, how is it?" I said, "It's fine, just get me up there." And when I got to the top, it was like the Fourth of July. I mean, it was an emotion like you can't even explain.

FLATHEAD:

While we were talking to them on the probe, they had asked us, "Do you realize how many people are up here?" I said, "There's probably going to be, you know, your normal rescue team." And they said, "There's thousands of people up here, and you're worldwide on TV." I relayed that message to the other guys. And it was like, "Holy shit."

When it was my turn to go, I grabbed the bit bucket with the notes we'd written in it. I wanted to be sure that we didn't leave that behind.

HARPO:

When I hit the surface and they pulled me out of the capsule and put me on the stretcher, I just heard people yelling, "Harpo, Harpo, Harpo!" I threw my hands up in the air and I said, "God bless America!" and then I was whisked off. They cut my clothes off of me faster than I could put them on and take them off myself, quickest bath I ever had in my life, too. It felt good.

BOOGIE:

I helped load the guys into the capsule. It was wet, water pouring down, we were getting drenched. I just throwed the guys in. Hound Dog is, like, "How the hell do you get in this thing?" Of course, he hadn't watched

Randy and Blaine, the first two guys who went up. None of them watched. They were bullshitting along the rib. So I opened the gate, swung around. And then there's a platform you fold down. I said, "Just get in." He got in headfirst. Most guys went in sideways. I said, "That's good," and I shut the gate. "Am I all right?" he asked. I said, "Yeah, put the headphones on." I told Moe, who was on the phone to the guys above, "Take him up, Moe." And he went up backwards.

HOUND DOG:

When them lights hit my eyes, it hurt. My pupils were big from that many days in the darkness and then getting out in that bright light, they just didn't get smaller, I guess. They were letting so much light in, I just barely could open my eyes, it was so blinding. When I got up there, I could see people, but I didn't recognize them or nothing. I have no idea who was there or anything when they helped me out of the cage.

They didn't ask me nothing. They took me in there, cut my clothes off clear down to my boots. Within thirty seconds, I was naked and they were hosing me off.

TUCKER:

When they grabbed us, there was no discussion—it was just like grabbing a kid when they're first born. They just cut your boots off and your underwear. I was a little nervous. I mean, they was down close to the privates there and they was whacking them. I said, "Buddy, whatever you do, just be a little careful because I ain't got much left down there."

At the firehouse, families gathered around the TV, watching the men being lifted out of the ground. After they had learned that their loved ones were alive, they had voted to allow the live broadcast of the event (had they decided against it, the rescue certainly would not have been broadcast— Governor Schweiker had left the final decision up to the families). After each man came up, someone at the rescue site would call over to the fire hall to let them know who was coming next, so that family members were sure not to miss it.

ANNETTE FOGLE:

I'm outside, waiting to hear who is coming when. My son Matthew told me that he'd come and get me. When I heard that the first guy up was going to be the one with chest pains, I thought that would be Tom [Tucker], because of his past history.

Then Matthew came running out, his hands waving, and he said, "They brought Dad out, they brought Dad out." And I looked at him and said, "Your dad's the one with chest pains?"

We were told they were flying him to Johnstown Hospital. A preacher came out and told us we could go, but to drive carefully. I wasn't too worried about the chest pains. After what we had been through, I figured we could deal with it.

MARGE MAYHUGH:

I was sitting there in the fire hall, and they announced that the second miner to come up would be "Wayne Davis." I had no idea who Wayne Davis was. There wasn't a Wayne Davis down there. They just screwed up.

Then they said, "Blaine Mayhugh." And it was, like, "Oh, my God."

The rescue went swiftly and smoothly. By 2:30 A.M. on Sunday, there were only two men left underground—Boogie and Moe.

SANDY POPERNACK:

I knew Mark [Moe] would be coming up last. I knew he wanted to make sure everybody was up. This guy behind me said, "I know it's going to be Boogie." I turned around and I said, "I bet you it's going to be Mark."

BOOGIE:

So it come down to me and Moe. I looked at Moe. I said, "Moe, go ahead up. I'll be okay." Moe looked at me and he said, "Bob, you go." I said, "No, you go." He said, "I'm okay." I said, "Are you sure? I ain't going to ask you twice. I'm getting out of here." He said, "Go ahead, I'll be all right." So I shook his hand. I said, "I'll see you upstairs." That's the last time I talked to Moe.

MOE:

After Boog left, I was alone down there. I took a look around. I cried a little bit then. I asked the guy on the radio, I wanted to make sure my wife and kids weren't up there—well, I couldn't make sure they weren't up there, but I didn't want them to be up there. Because I knew when I seen them I was going to lose it.

By then, I had a pretty good idea what was going on up on top. Every time somebody surfaced, it was just like being at the Super Bowl when somebody got a touchdown. I mean, you could hear them screaming, hollering, and clapping. When I got up there, I knew this was going to be a serious emotional problem.

While I was waiting for the cage to come down, it was really quiet. I've never felt anything like it in my life. This guy's talking to me on the radio and I just kind of, you know, I didn't even answer him. I could hear him saying, "Are you still there, are you still there?" I was just looking around, looking around at the mine, the gear we left down there . . . just reflecting. I was thinking this was maybe my last time in the mine. I looked at this stuff and I thought to myself, Man, I hope I never see anything like this again.

When the capsule came down, I got myself in, and they started pulling me up. As I was rising, I was looking at the strata—there's sand rock, there's slate. I've got my finger out, touching it. Water is pouring over me. I could hear the roar of the people above. I was just enjoying that last ride.

JOHN UNGER:

They life-flighted me and Randy Fogle down to Johnstown Hospital in a helicopter. Randy because of his heart, you know, and me because my shoulder was hurtin' pretty bad. On my flight, there was this really great nurse. After she had me all strapped in and my IV in place and everything, she said, "Can I get you anything else?" I said, "There's only one other thing I'd really like to have." And she said, "Whatever it is, you know if I have it, I'll do it for you."

I said, "I'd like to have a nice, soft, warm woman to hold right now."

She goes, "What?"

I said, "That's what I'd really like to have, just to hug a woman." She smiled. She said, "You spent seventy-seven hours in hell and the first thing you think about is a woman." I said, "Hey, that's not asking for too much, is it?"

And she laughed.

19 · REUNION

MISSY PHILLIPPI:

I was still at the rescue site, waiting for John [Flat-head] to come up. I couldn't see what was going on—I was just waiting out where the ambulances were, trying to keep out of the way. One of the rescue workers came up and said, "Is your husband bald?" And I didn't know how to answer because his hair's getting a little thin. But I was thinking, "Oh, my, what happened to his hair?" I said, "Well, not completely." And they said, "Never mind." I think they confused my husband with John Unger. I did chuckle a little bit.

Then one of the women on the ambulance crew said, "Missy, he's coming. Get ready." And I climbed in the back of the ambulance. I was only there for a minute, when they brought him in.

I had a hard time seeing him at first, because there was this seat between us. I went to lean up, and my seat belt stopped me, so I clicked it off. He was kinda rolling his head around, jerking a little bit. And they had him so covered with blankets, you know—I could see the IV line running down there, but I couldn't see anything else below his neck and shoulders.

I was afraid to touch him. They said something about his eyes, how they might be hurtin' from the light. I wasn't sure what to do. I said, "Can I touch you?" Because I was afraid because his head kept rolling around like that. And I didn't know why. He said, "Yeah." Then he started crying, and I started crying. And I put my hand on his head and leaned down close to him. I said, "You're never, ever, ever going to go through that again, never."

LESLIE MAYHUGH:

When I walked into the emergency room and first saw Blaine, he looked like hell. They hadn't put him nowhere yet, just right there behind a curtain. His face was drawn in and the color was bad. His hands were gray. He was cold, I mean like hypothermia cold. I'm a nurse. I've worked with people that were dying. And I knew his temperature was not right, not even close. His feet were gray and cold and had all these wrinkles from being in the water too long.

All I was allowed to do was grab his hand because they were giving him oxygen and doing all this other stuff with him, checking his temperature.

I reached down to kiss his hand. The first thing he said was, "It has to be a miracle that we made it out. If you only knew the stuff we went through." Of course, I had no clue. The second thing he said was, "I'm not going back in, ever." And I thought, Well, I never would make you. I'd never want you to. And the third thing he said was, "How are the kids holding up?"

Of course, I had to joke around, like, "Well, don't ask about me, that's okay . . ."

It wasn't until later that night that Blaine saw the kids. David, his nephew, brought him clothes and brought the kids up. They had a hard time getting through the media to get into the hospital.

When Blaine saw the children, they didn't act the way he thought they were going to act. They were excited, but they didn't show it because they thought he was gone. You know, they thought their dad was dead. They were sort of afraid to touch him at first. They heard he was going to be cold. They heard people talking about hypothermia, but they didn't know what the word was. So that first day or two, they weren't themselves at all. It sort of scared me. I think they were in shock for quite a while.

HARPO:

My wife and my two boys came to see me in the emergency room. They said, "Dennis, we all love you," and then my wife gave me a kiss. And she told my boys, "Give your dad a kiss." It was just a very happy moment in my life.

BOOGIE:

When I seen my family walk in, I bawled like a baby. That's the only time I cried. It was particularly hard when I seen my boy, Ben. He hugged me. He said, "Dad, promise me you won't go back to the mine."

I couldn't promise him. I didn't say, because I have to live and pay my bills. That's the only thing I know. He asked that twice, crying and hugging me. "Promise me you won't go back." I couldn't.

My girls, they didn't even make me promise. They just said, "Dad, you're not going back in that coal mine." And my girlfriend Cindy, she said straight out that she'd break up with me if I went back in the mine. She don't pull no punches.

UNGER:

When my family walked in, it was overwhelming. I was thinking I'd never see them again. My wife came in, then my son and daughter. There was a whole pile of people there to see me.

My wife said, "I never gave up. I just made up my

mind that I know what you're all about and if anybody was coming out, I knew you'd be there."

I said, "Well, I don't want to disappoint you, but there was a time in there that I wasn't sure I was going to get the job done that you thought I was going to be able to do."

But that's the way my wife is. She's a strong woman. I mean, what she endures. She is just a remarkable person. I've never met anybody as strong as she is.

ANNETTE FOGLE:

Randy had coal dirt in his ears, coal dirt under his nose, in his mustache. He had two pieces of cotton over his eyes to keep the light out.

The whole family went in, but then they just kind of backed off and left me to do what I had to do. So I went up there to say those three words I had forgotten to say to him that morning when he left.

"I love you," I told him. And I gave him a kiss.

I took my time, I held his hand, and then I let the kids come in. And my pastor came in and said a prayer. He sat with us and prayed with us and thanked God for their safe return.

On Sunday, while America celebrated their courage and their brotherhood, the miners slept. Randy, Tucker, Unger,

Flathead, Harpo, and Boogie were all at Conemaugh Memorial Medical Center in Johnstown; Blaine, Hound Dog, and Moe were at Somerset Hospital. It was a blissful day. They had spent more than seventy-seven hours in a tight, black, cold hole in the ground, and now they had been delivered to a warm, white hospital bed. All they wanted to do was grab a wad of chew, kiss their wives and children, and close their eyes for the next ten hours.

Governor Schweiker made the rounds, catching some of the miners between snoozes. By now, he and Blaine Mayhugh, Sr., were on a first-name basis—all the shouting and worry and second-guessing were forgotten.

TUCKER:

The governor came in there and he made me feel good. He said, "We'll take care of you. There ain't going to be no problems with anything." That was good to hear. We watched a little NASCAR together. The governor is a big fan, you know, and wants to do some racing himself. And like two laps into the race, there was a heck of a crash—Earnhardt and another guy plowed into the fence. I mean, cars went flying and rolling.

I said, "Now, why in the heck would you want to go and do something like that, get yourself killed?" He said, "I like driving race cars." And I said, "Well, buddy, good luck to you. I'll come down and watch you if I get a little time."

By late Sunday, Hound Dog, Harpo, Boogie, Flathead, Blaine, and Moe were all released. Given their ordeal, these guys were all in amazingly good shape. Many of them— especially Moe—still had some pain and numbness in their feet, but that would go away soon enough. They had all lost weight (Tucker dropped twelve pounds). Their skin was still soggy. Boogie had a badly bruised thumbnail where he had hit it with a hammer. But they were ready to go home and begin their lives again.

HOUND DOG:

The first night I come home, Cathy and I laid there in bed together and she wouldn't let go of me for about two hours. I almost forgot how good it felt.

Doctors were a little concerned about the pain in John Unger's shoulder. After being examined by Navy doctors, they decided he should undergo oxygen therapy in a hyperbaric chamber. That meant sitting in an airtight steel container for six hours while it was pressurized with oxygen, then slowly depressurized (a common treatment for excess nitrogen in the bloodstream, which causes the bends and can lead to a variety of serious health problems). Unger was not happy about being trapped again, even if it was only for a few hours. "I was hot and tired and real wore out. I just wanted to get out. But it did help my shoulder. It felt a lot better after that." He was released on Monday, and immediately went home to his eighty-acre farm outside of Somerset.

Both Tucker and Randy remained in the hospital for cardiac evaluations. On Sunday, Randy's heart began racing, at one point reaching 240 beats per minute—a development that for a few hours had doctors worried. But it turned out they were able to get it under control with drugs, and various tests showed his heart to be in fine working order—it was just a reaction to the tremendous stress he had been under. Randy was released late Monday.

Tucker was the last to go home. With his history of heart trouble, doctors wanted to be sure everything was in good working order. He underwent a stress test, echo-cardiograms, and a procedure to check for blocked arteries. Nothing alarming turned up, but they kept him around until Tuesday afternoon just to be sure.

When they arrived at home, every one of these men walked into a new world. Four or five days earlier, they had been simple coal miners, men who labor under incredibly difficult and dangerous conditions to put food on the table for their families—and, in a few cases, because they loved the work itself.

When they emerged from that 26-inch shaft in the

ground, they were different men. They met and shook hands with the president of the United States, who praised them for their "American spirit." Their faces and names were now known by millions of people around the world. They were celebrated for their camaraderie, their stamina, their survival skills, their common sense, and their just plain good luck. Offers came pouring in—box seats at Pittsburgh Steeler games, private jets to NASCAR races, and, yes, book and movie deals.

It was a big adjustment, and it would not be an easy one. In their future, there would be TV appearances, parades, parties at the governor's house, and Miss America pageants. But there would also be nightmares of water and drowning, a federal investigation into whether what happened in the Quecreek mine could have and should have been prevented, and worries about what they were going to do next in their lives (Governor Schweiker promised to help them in their job hunts).

Most of the guys have no plans to ever go back in a coal mine—and are damn happy about it. But for Randy and Moe, it's not so easy to say good-bye. They love the rough poetry of work underground. Despite what happened, they both want to figure out a way to put their many years of experience to good use, perhaps as mine inspectors or superintendents. But even Moe, a third-generation miner, is adamant that neither Daniel nor Lucas will ever work in a coal mine—"not that they'd ever want to after all this," Moe says. Like the other guys with young kids, Moe gets a little glassy-eyed as he thinks about how the trauma of this event will affect his kids' lives.

As for the farewell notes that were written in the mine, none of the guys have told their wives or families what they said. And they don't plan to, either. The bucket is in Randy's possession now, and he's taking very good care of it. Someday soon, he says, he will take it back down into the mine, right back up to the spot where Moe cut through. And he will place that bucket up in that old mine as far as he can reach, then the engineers will seal it up, entombing their most private thoughts written in their most desperate hour.

But on that hot July night when the nine miners finally emerged black-faced from the ground, all this was still in the future. What was important at that moment was simply the miraculous fact that they had gotten out, born again, with the rarest gift of all: their lives.

RANDY:

When I was in the hospital, I couldn't see the sun come up. I could see the daylight, but I couldn't see the sun. When I come home, I got up early that next morning. I went outside and sat out on my bench on the other side of my garage and read a book, a Tom Clancy novel. I wanted to watch the sun come up. It's something I thought I might never see again. Just that little thing, I mean, it happens every day. But when you're down in the darkness for a while, and you don't know if you're ever going to get out—well, you realize that little thing that happens every day, just the sun rising up over that hill, that's what it's all about.